James Greenwood

Legends of savage Life

James Greenwood

Legends of savage Life

ISBN/EAN: 9783337153625

Printed in Europe, USA, Canada, Australia, Japan

Cover: Foto ©ninafisch / pixelio.de

More available books at **www.hansebooks.com**

LEGENDS

OF

SAVAGE LIFE.

BY

JAMES GREENWOOD.

WITH THIRTY-SIX ILLUSTRATIONS, DRAWN ON WOOD, BY

ERNEST GRISET,

FROM HIS ORIGINAL DESIGNS.

LONDON:
JOHN CAMDEN HOTTEN, PICCADILLY.
1869.

	PAGE
1. Illustrated Title . . .	1
2. Heading to List of Illustrations . . .	5
3. Kaphoozlem declines to recognise her Grandson	10
4. This is Milkeekokum	11
5. The Hairy Spider shows his Attachment for Milkeekokum	19
6. The Hairy Spiders endeavour to take Milkeekokum captive	21
7. This is Milkeekokum and his Grandmother	31
8. Is it his Grandmother?	35
9. Milkeekokum continues the Pursuit of his Grandmother . .	39
10. This is the closest that Milkeekokum ever got to the "Great Charm"	41
11. Pynchbloo, Skrapeshyn, and Lupe at their Barbarous Supper .	45
12. This is how Swyvlgoggle was Lured to Destruction	49
13. The Wrong Fish . .	52
14. The Witch-Seal captured .	56

15. The Elk Demon receives his Coup-de-Grâce
16. Pitchanicker watching for his Totem
17. Pitchanicker pursues the Elk Man
18. The Elk Demon at Bay
19. Pitchanicker Wins the Second Trick
20. The Djujube Family at Tiffin after their Sea Voyage
21. Djujube sets out to Fish for his expected Friends
22. The Escape from Black Stone Island
23. Djujube tries his Hand as a Huntsman on the wonderful Island
24. Terrible Shifts of the Djujube Family
25. The Last of his Race
26. The Black Stone Priest recovers the Magic Stone
27. The Miracle of the Enchanted Spear
28. Djujube's Last Appearance in Life
29. The Whoggles successfully Invade the Whangs
30. Dance before Meat, as performed by the Monsters of the Cave
31. Audacious Reception of the Whoggle Commissioners by the Whangs
32. The Whangs perform a Lamentation Dance on the Loss of the Clay Head
33. The Living Tomb of the Clay Head is Brought Ashore
34. The Irresistible Charge of the Votaries of the Clay Head
35. The Last Occasion of the Whoggles Picking a Bone with their Enemies
36. Final Appearance of the Heads of this Tale

Engraved by H. N. Woods.

GRANDMOTHER WASP.

KAPHOOZLEM DECLINES TO RECOGNISE HER GRANDSON.

GRANDMOTHER WASP.

THIS IS MILKEEKOKUM.

WITHOUT doubt he must be mad. Who else but a man bereft of his senses would perch his house on four legs, each taller than the legs of an ostrich? Who else but a poor creature who through some great misfortune had come to have no more brains than a monkey, would be at such pains to make him a home up in the air, as monkeys build their nests in the topmost branches of the palm, exposed to the high wind, and the thick of the rain, and the unscreened rays of the blazing sun? Hottentots of sense smoke their pipes in the shade; this one mounts the roof of his castle in the air and there sits baking till the perspiration trickling down the fingers that grasp the pipe-stem bids fair to put the fire out. He must be mad, or an idiot at the very least.

So you would have thought, my children, if, ignorant of who he was, you had seen him. You would have pitied the lonely wretch squatted atop of his lofty hut in the wilderness, and unslinging your water-skin would have invited him down to refresh himself with a cool draught; and if, as would certainly have been the case, he had replied to your civil invitation by abusing you in a most frightful manner and pelting you with stones, of which he was never without a large supply concealed in the folds of his loin-cloth, you would have felt no offence, but, attributing such strange conduct to his insanity, passed on commiserating him more than ever. And yet, my children, although the wisest and safest course were to pass on and leave him, in deeming him mad you were never more mistaken in all your lives.

Never did there exist since the world was made a man more crafty and cunning than Milkeekokum; never was there a wickeder man. Ambition was his ruin. Amongst the Kybobs, to which tribe he belonged, he might have lived honoured and respected by all who knew him, for his knowledge of medicine and charms to cure all manner of diseases was almost equal to that of that wise old witch doctor Djrydydlyr, who likewise was a rainmaker, and while the youthful Milkeekokum was still tending his father's cattle in the kraal, it was whispered that the day would come when he would take Djry's place and rank amongst the tribe second in importance only to the chief himself. Milkeekokum could already make rain in small quantities, and this, as you know, is a witch doctor's chief power. Whether it was true, as Djrydydlyr asserted, he had come prying about his hut on occasions when he was engaged in brewing rain for the thirsty people, and had so got an inkling of the process, cannot be vouched with certainty, but this much is beyond doubt: while the land was parched and the dry tongues of the cattle hung out of their mouths for want of a drink, and the regular rainmaker was sweating night and day through his prodigious exertions to "make downpour," Milkeekokum had been known to disappear for a few hours and return looking brisk and lively, and with all the dust washed from his skin and his wool wet to its roots. When they questioned him he laughed and made light of the matter, but there was no doubt that he had betaken himself to a secluded spot in the forest and there made for himself a quiet little shower, enough to suit his present necessities. He denied it, however, and as he was invariably accompanied by his grandmother on these strange excursions, he would appeal to her, and she too would laugh and declare that herself and her grandson had been out digging for black ants, of which, when fried in the fat of the butternut, she was passionately fond. "I cannot dig for myself," said the old woman; "my arms are now too feeble to wield the digging-stick, but my grandson is vigorous and obedient, and his strong arms never tire." "But how comes his skin so clean? What makes his wool so wet?" they asked. "It is the tears of gratitude I shed over my kind grandson that makes his wool wet," the old woman answered, "and it is cheerfulness at having performed a charitable act towards his grandmother that gives him that fresh and lively look which you mistake for refreshing by rain." Had she not been so highly respected amongst the Kybobs, it is likely that her explanation would have been not altogether satisfactory; but the implicit reliance these people place in their elders is well known all the world over. "Come here, my son, and let me embrace thee," said Djrydydlyr to the young Milkeekokum, and while he did so he applied his tongue to the youth's wool and discovered that the moisture was *fresh*, whereas, if its source had been the old woman's tears, it would most likely have been *salt*. But Djry was fully six years and a-half the junior of Milkeekokum's grandmother, and therefore he durst not open his mouth.

And quite true it was that there existed between Milkeekokum and his grandmother a friendship of a warmth not ordinarily found between such relatives, even amongst the affectionate Kybobs. But it was a friendship based on grounds the tribe in general never so much as dreamt of. It was a secret. This was the secret:—

The family of which Milkeekokum was the youngest descendant was the longest-lived of its own or of any surrounding tribe. As has already been stated, Kaphoozlem, Milkeekokum's grandmother, was six years and a-half older than the witch doctor Djrydydlyr, and he was known to have been ninety-seven last birthday. It was on the female side that this longevity was chiefly remarkable, for although Milkeekokum's mother, owing to some little misunderstanding she had with his father, died at an early age, his great-grandmother—the mother of Kaphoozlem, that is—and her mother before her, arrived at an age with which the age of Kaphoozlem was comparatively childish. There was a mystery about the death of Kaphoozlem's mother. It had been her custom to make her way into the forest every morning as soon as she rose from her grass bed, and to stay there a little while and then return. It was to give her an appetite for her breakfast, she said, nothing more nor less, but that was not strictly true. *It was to seek the means wherewith to prolong her life* that she paid her matutinal visits to the thicket. It was proved to be so, for one morning she returned looking, not blithe and buxom as was her wont, but long-visaged and haggard, and so weak that she could scarcely stagger to the hut where her eldest daughter, Kaphoozlem, resided. She did manage to reach it, however, but had not her daughter been just within the doorway as she entered, she would assuredly have fallen to the earth.

"What ails my mother?" inquired Kaphoozlem, catching the fainting form of her aged parent in her arms.

"Oh, Kaph!" groaned the old woman, "it is all over with me! It was the same with my own poor mother, and yet I could not take warning from her last words. O-o-o-oh!"

Poor Kaphoozlem was bewildered.

"Explain yourself, my parent," said she. "What was the warning that you should have minded and did not? In what respect was it with my respected grandmother as it is now with you?"

"Listen, Kaph!" gasped the old woman: "the sun in its glory is like the round ripe fruit of the bullyboo; then the life-lengthener that lives in the forest hides its head, and may not be spoken with; but when the sun has but just got up, and his head shines up in the shape of a pot-lid, then the life-lengthener is bold, and may be met and dealt with by such as know how to find him. Alas! why should we who have the secret ever be so weak as to oversleep ourselves? Why did my mother? Why did *her* mother? Why did I this unlucky morning?"

And once more the old woman, as she squatted on the floor, rocked to and fro, and howled in a manner that was heartrending to hear. As for Kaphoozlem, she had heard sufficient to make her anxious to hear more. What was this life-lengthener her mother had spoken of? Was it in search of it that she went to the forest every morning, and was it that, previously to this morning, she had always been successful in finding it that accounted for her great age? Hark! her mother is now mumbling as well as moaning.

"Why, why did I not use diligence, and run when I found the sun was so high? Then I might have tasted of it once again, and again, and ever again, and never have died!"

Kaphoozlem's suspicions were confirmed. What her mother went to seek in the forest was a charm against death.

"Tell me, my mother," said she, embracing her parent, who each moment was growing weaker—"tell me the name of this life-lengthener; tell me its shape, and how it may be found."

"Bend thine ear, my daughter, and I will tell thee, and thou must keep the secret until thy daughter reaches the age of a hundred years, and then thou mayest reveal it."

"Yes, yes, but the name—the shape?" urged Kaphoozlem impatiently, as she saw that her mother's breath was failing.

"The name of the life-lengthener, my daughter, is——"

It was a hard name seemingly, judging from the ugly face the old woman made in endeavouring to give utterance to it—so hard, indeed, that it stuck in her throat and choked the little life remaining in her; and without any further word or sign she fell back dead.

At this time Kaphoozlem was in her seventieth year, and not unnaturally was occasionally troubled with serious thoughts as to her latter end. Scarcely a woman of the tribe ever attained an age beyond hers at present, and though through several generations the women of her family had lived very many years longer, there was no security that she should not be an exception to the rule, and, as just observed, the reflection at times made her very miserable. This revelation of her mother's, however, as far as it went, filled her heart with strange emotions. Without doubt the secret of the longevity of the females of her family consisted in their acquaintance with this life-lengthener, whatever it was. What could it be? As she sat by her mother's body she scrutinised the shape of its mouth closely, speculating what word would best fit it. So desperately anxious was she to get at the word so nearly spoken that she pressed against the chest of her dead mother with a sort of hope that the precious word might be even yet lingering, and wanting but a little assistance to escape. But she might as well have pressed her husband's bellows for a reply (her husband was a blacksmith). And so, without saying a word of the old woman's last words, she called in her neighbours, and her mother was carried out and decently buried.

But Kaphoozlem could not rest contented, the more so as she day by day discovered that worrying and pondering over the word which was the key to the grand secret was wearing her out and killing her before her time. The life she led was pitiable. Every morning, soon as the first grey of morning appeared, she was up and off to the forest, but when she got there she would have been as well at home, since she had no more idea than the man in the moon—not so much, indeed, and in all probability—what to look for. She didn't know even whether this life-lengthener was dead or alive—whether it took the shape of a tree, or a snake, or an ant, or a hippopotamus. It was worse than hunting with one's eyes shut for a diamond lost on a dusty road. It made her miserable. She lodged with Milkeekokum's father, who by this time had married a second wife, and when she came home from her fruitless journey the second wife would say, "Been to seek an appetite for breakfast, granny?" meaning it kindly enough, but as she repeated it every morning the old woman detected something like chaff in the inquiry, and in the bitterness of her heart wished that when she did discover this root, or whatever it was, of life, she might at the same time stumble on the root of death, in which latter case she would behave with great liberality towards her daughter-in-law.

At last, and in an evil hour, she confided the secret that was weighing on her so heavily to her young grandson Milkeekokum. As before stated, he was a youth of very superior intelligence, and wise far beyond his years. Besides which, he was active as a monkey and very strong, which qualities the old woman had not overlooked when making up her mind to take him into her confidence. "For all I know," she reasoned, "the life-lengthener may be in the shape of a lizard that lives under the roots of a tree; if so, with his ironwood spade in his strong young hands, he will be able to dig him out; or it may be that the life-lengthener lodges up in a tree in a bird's nest; if so young Milkeekokum will be able to climb and find it, and that before the sun rises full and round as the fruit of the bullyboo, whereas, if I attempted to search in this direction, by the time my stiff old limbs had carried me to the top of the tree the sun would have passed clean over my head."

So she up and told Milkeekokum all about it, in the first place, however, making him swear a great number of the most terrible oaths in the Hottentot language that under no circumstances would he reveal her secret. To be sure, since his grandmother had made such a fuss about it, he was not a little disappointed that there should be so very little to reveal, and only that the old woman appeared so mightily earnest in the matter, and, moreover, she was his grandmother, it is not impossible that he would have laughed at her. But this was only at first. When he began to reflect on the matter, the importance of her communication became more and more apparent to him. He could not forget the fact that his grandmothers, as far back as the history of the Kybobs extended, had lived to be extraordinarily old—were in a fair way towards living for ever when they died. Was it impossible that accident only had frustrated their intentions in every instance? It was not impossible.

Again, would not the secret, even though the search after it occupied months and even years, repay the trouble? When the ambitious Milkeekokum took this view of it, when he pictured himself armed with a means of preserving his life against the heaviest odds that might be brought against it—against the witch doctor and his poison ordeals, against the chief and all the clubs and spears at his command, his young blood coursed through his veins at a rate that set him skipping for joy, and yelling exultantly as though the grand end were already accomplished.

At length he grew calm, and enjoined his grandmother to explain minutely her last conversation with her mother, and how close she had come to uttering the most desirable word. She told him, nay, she went beyond, and, as well as she was able, put her shrivelled lips into shape such as her mother's were when the breath left her body, that her grandson might give a guess as to what the unuttered word might have been. But Milkeekokum could make nothing of this, since the lips were merely screwed up tight, rather as though, while life remained in her, the old woman had determined that the word should not be spoken than as if it were inadvertently nipped in the delivery.

"She could not have said anything with her mouth like that, grandmother," said the young man. "It is so many years ago that perhaps you forget."

This made the old woman angry.

"I recollect," she replied, "as though it were yesterday—as though it were but an hour since:—' The name, my daughter, of the life-lengthener is——' And then she made a little hissing noise like ' *i-s-s-s-p*,' and then she died with her mouth in the shape I show you."

"Then you think that the word was half said, grandmother?"

"Either so, or the noise was the hissing of her breath as it was leaving her."

Milkeekokum pondered a few moments, and then an idea seemed suddenly to occur to him; but so that his sharp-eyed old grandmother might not suspect it from the involuntary lighting up of his countenance, he turned away his head, remarking—

"Ay, ay! no doubt it was the hissing of her breath as it left my poor great-grandmother's body. It is growing late now; we will talk further of the matter to-morrow."

It would, perhaps, be more correct to say that two ideas, both of which he was desirous of concealing, had occurred to Milkeekokum as he sat pondering the word that his dying great-grandmother had screwed up her mouth to make. The first idea was that he had a clue to the mystery, and the second idea was, that if so, it was his own clue to follow up or leave as he pleased, and that if he chose to be at the trouble of following it up, he was entitled to the fullest benefit of it, to the exclusion of everybody else.

"If there's two in the secret, and the second one a woman, it will miscarry, without doubt; it *has* miscarried after a certain point ever since it was intrusted to the first woman of our tribe who was favoured with it. We'll have no more bungling. If I find out this charm, I'll keep it to myself. Most likely there are two of a sort; if so, my grandmother is very welcome to discover the other."

And so the ungrateful fellow walked off, grinning, and softly saying "I-s-s-s-p, i-s-s-s-p" to himself, each time with more satisfaction.

"It isn't 'i-s-s-s-p' at all, it is 's-s-s-p' without the 'i.' It is as clear as water what the word was to be. What is there to be met in the woods beginning s-s-p? Only one thing, and that is a witch thing, that roams abroad at night and clicks in the thatch and frightens you when you lie abed. It is the spider! I always thought that the spider was a strange fellow at spinning. I am convinced it must be the spider, the great hairy spider that builds his house in the sand, that my great-grandmother went to see every morning, so that he might spin out her life a day longer and a day longer. I will go out to-morrow morning and learn all about it."

Little sleep did Milkeekokum get that night. Before daybreak he was out, taking his spear with him, so that any one abroad so early might suppose that he was going a-hunting; and after walking a distance of five miles, he came to the sandy parts where the hairy spiders burrow. They are the largest spiders in the world those of the Kybob country, equalling in size full-grown crabs, and of such ferocious disposition that a brace of them have been known to frighten an ostrich off her nest, the invaders instantly taking possession of the eggs, cracking them with their fore-paws, and sucking them dry.

Under ordinary circumstances Milkeekokum, although as plucky a young fellow as ever walked, would scarcely have found courage to invade the territory of the ravening monsters; but he buoyed up his spirits with the reflection that, in the first place, his visit to them was one of a friendly nature, and that if, as he suspected, they were the holders of the charm, they would in all probability be rather glad than otherwise to renew friendly relations with a member of the favoured family; and, in the second place, the prize to be won was of a nature worth risking something very considerable to attain. So with a light heart, and a shrewd eye to the right and the left of him, he journeyed on until he spied a crevice which bore evidences of being inhabited by the insects of which he was in search.

How to rouse their attention was the next thing to be considered. It would have been easy enough to accomplish it by digging his spear into the hole, but the very last of his desires was to give offence; so he abandoned the notion as soon as it occurred to him.

THE HAIRY SPIDER SHOWS HIS ATTACHMENT FOR MILKEEKOKUM.

He stamped, and coughed, and "hemmed" for fully five minutes without any apparent result. By this time the sun was peeping up in the east, and he resolved to waste no more time; so lying down flat he applied his mouth to the crevice, and in the most civil and persuasive tones begged of any hairy spider that might happen to be below to step up and answer him a question or two.

Never was there a more prompt and signal instance of the danger of poking a nose where it is unwelcome. Scarcely had Milkeekokum concluded his polite speech than his nasal organ was afflicted with a sudden and frightful pain, as though the blades of a pair of red-hot tongs had seized it. With a terrific yell he leaped to his feet, dragging up with him a hairy spider of monstrous size, that held on to his nose with its hideous claws, causing him the most exquisite agony as it swung to and fro. Now indeed their mouths were close enough together to have admitted of the most confidential conversation; but such were Milkeekokum's sufferings that the purport of his errand was quite put out of his head, and his hot Hottentot blood being roused, his only thought was how to take vengeance on his enemy. How, if ever, he would have accomplished his design, is hard to say, had he not suddenly bethought him of his spear, which he had placed on the ground when he lay down to apply his mouth to the crevice. Catching it up, in imminent danger of piercing through the gristle of his snout as well, he transfixed the hairy demon, and with the deadliest hatred flashing from his eyes, held it aloft.

But, alas! the young man's triumph was of but short duration. While his enemy was still kicking at his spear-head, he suddenly felt a strange sensation about his feet, and looking down, to his horror and amazement discovered that two relatives of his first aggressor were busy at work avenging its untimely end. The threads spun by these gigantic creatures are stout as whipcord and almost as tough, and there they were weaving them about his feet and hauling them tight, evidently with the dreadful intention of taking him prisoner, and binding him so that he might be devoured at their leisure; and all the time they were whistling at the top of their voices, doubtless to call further assistance of their fellows living in the neighbourhood.

Milkeekokum was frantic with fright. At the rate they were weaving and tying, even of their individual exertions the two spiders would presently overcome him, unless he made a tremendous effort, and how would he fare if an army of the terrible monsters set on him? The horrid thought lent to his limbs the strength of three men. Flinging aside his spear, he made a prodigious leap up into the air, the cords were snapped, and the young Kybob was free. How he reached his hut he never knew, since so soon as the feat was accomplished, fatigue and the pain of his nose conquered him, and sinking on to his bed he fainted away.

To such an alarming extent was Milkeekokum's nose swollen when he awoke out of his swoon, that he might have remained in it for all he could see out of his eyes; while he was endeavouring to rouse himself and recollect the terrible events of the early morning, who should step in but his grandmother.

He could not see the old woman, but he knew her voice at once, and unjustly attributing his misfortune to her, could scarce sufficiently restrain his rageful feelings to answer civilly her wondering inquiry as to what he had been doing with his nose. He was cunning enough, however, to conceal the facts of the case, and simply replied that he knew nothing at all about it, some insect must have stung him while he slept, he supposed.

THE HAIRY SPIDERS ENDEAVOUR TO TAKE MILKEEKOKUM CAPTIVE.

"But there is a wound on each side of it ever so big," said his grandmother. "Ah, that is where I must have scratched it with my finger-nails when, in my sleep, I put up my hand to catch the thing," replied Milkeekokum; "if you've got anything to apply to it that will take the swelling down, it will give me much more comfort than talking about it."

So his grandmother went out and presently came back with some herbs, the leaves of which she broke up and made into a poultice, which gave him ease so speedily that he inquired what the leaves were.

"That is a secret," replied his grandmother; "my mother was a herb-wise woman, and so I am, but not so wise as she was. I've heard her say that there was nothing in the world that herbs would not cure if we only knew how to use them."

"Did she say that? did she say that there was nothing in the world that herbs would not cure if you only knew how to use them?" asked Milkeekokum with assumed indifference, but at the same time opening one of his puffy eyes wider than seemed possible a moment before.

"I have heard her say so a hundred times," replied his grandmother; "she used to chew herb-leaves very often."

"What sort of herb-leaves?" asked Milkeekokum, affecting to chafe his nose, but all the while watching his grandmother narrowly through his fingers.

"Ah, that's another secret," replied the old woman, "and one that I cannot reveal because I am ignorant of it. My mother never would tell me, never would let me see the leaves even. Once I found some leaves hidden in a chink in the wattle, just where her bed was, but they couldn't have been of the sort that she chewed, because, although it is so many years since that I can't recollect the kind, I know that they were poison-leaves."

At this Milkeekokum uttered a soft and prolonged whistle, which luckily for him his grandmother mistook for an indication of the pain his nose was causing him, and as soon as he perceived this he took to rocking to and fro on his bed and groaning in a very dismal manner.

"You will be the better for a few hours' sleep, my grandson," said the old woman. "I will leave you. Shut your eyes, dear, and try to compose yourself."

Milkeekokum promised that he would, but so far from closing his eyes, soon as his aged relative had turned her back he opened them particularly wide, and in a softer key repeated the whistle he had involuntarily given utterance to a minute before.

"So *that* is how the wind blows, eh?" chuckled he, his little eyes looking all the more malicious and diabolic from being set so far in his head. "I was a fool for being so hasty with my conclusion as to what 's-s-p' was the beginning of. It is not a spider that this life-lengthener lives in, it is in a herb. P'r'aps it is hyssop! My great-grandmother was as ignorant as my grandmother, I'll wager, and would be just as careless of her *h*'s. She would call it ''issop!' There you get the 's-s-s' at once. Stay a moment, though: all the tribe take hyssop at some time or another, and they don't all live for ever. No, it cannot be hyssop. Besides, the hidden leaves were those of a *poison* herb. Or rather," continued Milkeekokum, recklessly smiting his injured nose with his forefinger, as an uncommonly brilliant idea occurred to him, "a herb that has the character of being poisonous *and is not!* That is the security of the secret, I have not the least doubt. The herb is thought to be poisonous—perhaps the most poisonous that grows—and no one except he has a knowledge of its true properties will dare touch it!"

Milkeekokum could always reflect on and mature a scheme to greater advantage when his eyes were closed. He closed them now, and only for the occasional twitching of his ugly features, or a sardonic grin that for an instant bared his teeth as another knot in the difficulty straightened before the ingenuity of his fertile brain, you would have thought him fast asleep. When, however, at the expiration of an hour or thereabout, he opened his eyes, it would have struck you at once that if he *had* been sleeping he had likewise been dreaming, and that his dreams had been of a very frightful character. The Evil One himself with a swollen nose could not have appeared more hideous, only that there was an air of bumptiousness and confidence about Milkeekokum that the Evil One never wears, since he knows of old experience that sin at its soundest is no more stable than a dried poppy.

Not but that the Evil One must have been very proud of the young Kybob as he beheld him and knew every one of the thoughts that had puffed him up to so mighty an idea of himself. While Milkeekokum lay with his eyes closed he had matured a plan that, poor silly creature, he thought must infallibly lead to the great success for which he yearned. The more he considered the matter the more he became convinced that the secret of the life-lengthener was to be found in a herb that passed as a poison herb. But how to arrive at the right one? To collect and test them one by one himself would be the act of a fool, since, supposing there to be twenty poison herbs growing, it was exactly nineteen to one that he killed himself at the first trial. Were there twenty sorts? He reckoned them up, and found the number to be twenty-three. He then reckoned up the number of his relatives including his grandmother, and by an extraordinary coincidence, and one from which he augured well, he discovered that it exactly tallied with the number of poison herbs. Under such a happy condition of circumstances his course was perfectly clear. He would collect *all* the herbs, and by some means convey a prepared dose of each to a relative, and carefully note the effect. If the person to whom the dose was administered died, then it would be certain that *that* was not the herb his great-grandmother used to chew, and so on, until he discovered the herb in which the grand secret dwelt, and he could not fail to do so since the lucky partaker of it would be not at all affected.

Shaky as he was still from his encounter with the hairy spiders, his impatience was too great to admit of delay, and there and then he went out with his grass-cloth bag over his shoulder, as though bent on gathering berries and roots. He went to the forest, and he plucked the herbs to the full number of twenty-three, tying each little bundle of leaves separately, so that there might be no chance of a mistake, and by the evening he had returned to his hut again.

Though his heart was so terribly wicked he still entertained considerable affection for his grandmother, and therefore resolved that she should have the fullest chance to preserve her life by giving her the broadest field to run in. She should be first, he decided, and further to favour her he selected the herb popularly believed to be the most virulent, "for," argued Milkeekokum, comforting his still sore nose with the tip of his forefinger, "it is nearly certain that the charm in its wisdom would choose for its habitation a house least suspected of any."

When it grew dusk his kind grandmother came again to him to inquire after his health, and to bring him some nice mutton-broth kept hot in an ostrich egg.

"Drink this, my grandson," said she; "you must make haste to get well, you know, and then we will set out together and find the life-lengthener."

"I had a dream after you left me this morning, my grandmother," answered the hypocrite, at the same time embracing her. "We may be nigher the great discovery than you think."

"Tell me the dream, Milkee," said the old woman coaxingly, and trembling in her eagerness. "I can, as you know, interpret dreams with any man or woman of the tribe. Tell it me, my grandson, and I will make it as clear as thy image reflected in a pool."

"Nay," replied Milkeekokum, "I cannot eat and talk at the same time, and if I pause to tell you my dream the broth will grow cold." And he went on with the broth, blowing it and sipping it deliberately.

"That is the worst of broth in an ostrich egg," observed the old woman petulantly; "it takes so long a time to eat it, it is so hot."

"It is best hot, my grandmother, and such good broth should not be wasted. Have some; it will be the sooner got rid of, and I can commence to tell my wonderful dream."

Under other circumstances his old grandmother would have scorned to touch a drop of the brew she had made for her favourite Milkeekokum, but now, burning with desire to hear about the dream, she consented to help him with the broth. So he got up and fetched a calabash, and pouring a fair half of his supper into it bade her "eat and welcome."

And, never dreaming of treachery, the old woman lapped up the broth with a relish that led Milkeekokum to think that he had indeed hit on the charmed herb at the first attempt, for before his grandmother came in he had carefully prepared the calabash by well rubbing the inside of it with a strong essence of the poison.

"Does it not seem to you that this broth has a strange flavour?" he asked, just to try her.

"It has a proper flavour, my grandson," she replied; "what other could it have since I made it?" And so saying she drained the calabash to the very last drop of broth in it.

But Milkeekokum lingered over his. The truth was he had no dream to tell, and all the while that he was leisurely sipping he was busy inventing something that should pass muster as a dream. At last he finished his broth, and pushing away the vessel that had contained it, began—

"The dream that came into my head this morning, good grandmother——"

But he got no further. Rising to her feet, with a face that had faded from pure black to a sickly ash colour, the old woman observed—

"Not to-night, Milkee, my dear; I feel strangely unwell, and will get home and go to bed. Good-night, grandson."

And hastily kissing him, and bestowing on him an embrace loving and lingering, as though the poor old thing had a presentiment of what was about to happen, she tottered away and left him.

What did Milkeekokum? Did he hasten after her, and, confessing his crime, beg her forgiveness ere she died? Not he. Since the moment when the hairy spider had gripped him by the nose his heart had hardened to the density of stone. His countenance even wore an expression of satisfaction as the old woman went out.

"I am a grandmother the poorer, but I have a doubt the less on my mind, which at least makes the matter square," soliloquised the ruffian; and then he lit his pipe and lay enjoying it till he fell asleep.

It did not in the least surprise him when next morning they brought him news that his grandmother was dead. Neither was he at all dismayed when the morning following he was informed that his uncle Walkahooki, who had looked in on the previous evening to discuss the question of mourning, had also given up the ghost. The whole tribe might have learnt resignation from the young Kybob's behaviour. Aunts, cousins, father and stepmother, fell like leaves in autumn, and there was every prospect of his presently finding himself bereft of every one of his kindred; but he heard of their departure as calmly as though they had only set out on a little journey and might shortly be expected back again. They did not know the secret that upheld him under his affliction; with every relative a doubt died; till at the expiration of five weeks he had but two cousins and a sister-in-law left, and an exactly similar number of doubts, in shape of as many little bundles of poison-leaves, which were carefully concealed in the earth under where his bed was.

At the expiration of another week the last of Milkeekokum's relatives were buried, but still to the young man's dismay it was as though with the last death all his doubts had sprung to life again. The great secret was still undiscovered. Clearly it was all a mistake as to the poison herbs, and bitterly did he reproach his defunct grandmother for misleading him into all the crimes he had committed during the last six weeks. The worst of it was, that the members of the tribe began to look suspiciously on him. Fully expecting that he too would die, when they found that he exhibited no symptoms of doing so, they took to whispering and shaking their heads. True, nothing could be brought against him— Milkeekokum's cunning and his knowledge of physics had effectually guarded against that — till the circumstance of his being left when all his kith and kin were snatched away, undoubtedly showed that he was marked out by the gods for *some* purpose, and since he could not show that that was a good purpose, he could scarcely grumble whatever their opinion might be. However, they did not hurt him; they simply declined to have anything to do with him. They would neither hunt with him, nor sit and smoke with him, nor keep his company in any sort of way. They were civil to him, but plainly enough intimated that they should regard it as a favour if for the future he kept himself to himself.

Proud as he was cruel and ambitious, Milkeekokum was not slow to take the hint. "Why should I crave the society of these wooden-heads?" said he; "I am not so poor that I need beg my bread of them; nay, thanks to my poor father's little property and the eight sheep my grandmother bequeathed me, I can get on pretty comfortably without working or begging either. Besides, if I am all alone I shall be the better able to give more strict attention to the discovery of this life-lengthening charm; for to discover it I am determined, or I will perish in the attempt."

So, gathering his portables, and investing what he got for the eight sheep his grandmother had left him in tobacco, he made his way deep into the forest, and there he built him his house on four legs, just as it is to be seen in the picture. To climb up to the roof of his house of afternoons, and, straddled like a tailor, there indulge in the Indian weed, was the greatest bliss he knew. To his mind there were several advantages in being perched up at such a height. In the first place, it was breezy and healthy; in the second place, it was fine to look down on the forest where the charm was, and to know that although you could not at present discover it, it was under your eye; and in the third place, although the wicked Kybob was *nearly* certain, yet he was not quite, that something might even yet turn up to point to him as the murderer of his relatives, and it might be as well to have a fair look-out on the road his accusers were likely to come.

Still, and despite this last little anxiety, he was very comfortable, and the more he became so, the more uncomfortable was the feeling that it could not last—that even though he remained unmolested on his happy perch in the wilderness, he must one day tumble and fall to the earth like a dead-ripe gooseberry. He got no sleep of nights through thinking about it, and very often when he did succeed in snatching forty winks, he would gradually recover consciousness under the impression that a wasp or a beetle had somehow found its way into his bedroom, but presently to discover that it was from his own lips that that ever-haunting sound of "s-s-s-p" proceeded. It was fortunate that the unlucky letters were but two of a healthy family of twenty-six; the way in which Milkeekokum twisted and tortured them was enough to undermine the constitution of a weaker alphabet.

One afternoon, squatting on his roof and just wakeful enough to keep his pipe alight, he heard this wearying "s-s-s-p," "s-s-s-p," more distinctly than ever he had since his grandmother had uttered it. This roused him to complete wakefulness, and he opened and shut his mouth several times to be quite sure that it was not himself that was making the sound. Then he leant his head and inclined it to the thatch, and the noise was louder than ever.

"It *is* a wasp this time!" exclaimed Milkeekokum, much irritated at being disturbed; "I wish it would come out here."

And scarcely had he said the words when the "s-s-s-p" ceased, giving place to a slight rustling sound just between where his legs were crossed, and presently the grass of the thatch at that spot separated, and a something no larger than a wasp poked up its head.

It was not a wasp, however, it was Kaphoozlem, Milkeekokum's grandmother. Small as was the face—no bigger, indeed, than a millet-seed—the features were perfect. There was even a wart on the chin, just as the old woman had worn it while in human shape. She had wasp's wings, and a wasp's body, and wasp's legs, and, quivering at her extremity, the sting of a wasp.

Milkeekokum might have been knocked from his perch with an ostrich feather, and trembled so that his pipe fell from his lips to the ground. For several moments he stared in dumb affright at the apparition, but finding that the expression of its countenance grew even less ferocious under his steady gaze, and that the quivering of its sting ceased entirely, he plucked up courage to address it.

"A pretty thing you've done for me, making me break my pipe, mistress wasp! If it wasn't for your striking likeness to my dear departed grandmother, who scalded herself to death through drinking hot broth, I'd crack you like a May bug. I'd advise you to be off while you are safe and sound."

To his great amazement, the wasp answered him in his grandmother's voice, and in terms quite mild and gentle—

"Not only am I like your grandmother, my dear Milkee, but so I *am*. It is true, and as you say, that my supposed death was caused through drinking scalding broth, but by virtue of the charm you put in it I did not die: I only changed my shape."

Milkeekokum stared wider-eyed than ever now. It was true, after all, then, that the charm lived in the poison herb—in the identical herb he had administered to Kaphoozlem. There had been odd times when he regretted the old woman's death. She used to provide him in many comforts he now missed, and now that he found that she had not been really dead at all, he felt somewhat sold.

"So all the time I have been weeping and lamenting your rash act you have been flying about and enjoying yourself," he moodily remarked.

"I have been flying about, and hopping about, and running about, but chiefly I have been roaring about," replied the tiny creature.

"Wasps do not roar," remarked Milkeekokum.

"But lions do."

"Lions!"

"A lion is my present proper shape," said the translated grandmother, "but I assumed the figure of a wasp that I might more easily reach you in your nest here. Sometimes I take the form of a hippopotamus when the sun is very hot and I feel inclined for a swim;

or of cold mornings I have taken ostrich shape, and indulged in a nice swift gallop. But I like being a lion best. It is a curious sensation to feel so big and powerful after being so long as a feeble old woman."

Milkeekokum's head was filled with the most conflicting thoughts. It seemed scarcely less remarkable that his grandmother should become a lion or a wasp than that she should be in ignorance of the trick he had put on her, and which caused her to quit her human shape.

"What made your sting start and quiver so when you first saw me?" he presently inquired.

"What other way had I as a wasp of expressing my joy at seeing you?" replied the creature. "Had I been in lion shape when we met I should have wagged my tail. It is exactly the same thing."

"You would not have lashed your tail?"

"Why should I, my dear grandson? To lash my tail would be to betray anger. Why should I be angry with one who all through my human life never treated me with aught but affection?"

"That is true," said Milkeekokum, laughing to himself to think that his grandmother was as big a fool as ever. Then, after a pause, he remarked—

"But have you merely come to see me and say good-bye, grandmother?"

"Nay, my grandson, I have come to reward you for your attention to me while I was an old woman. I have come to tell you how you may become any shape that may please you, and live for ever and ever."

"That is exactly what I should like," promptly answered Milkeekokum. "How am I to set about it?"

"The process seems difficult, but really nothing can be more simple," replied the wasp. "I have no power to help you but in my lion shape. In that shape you must seek me and conquer me, or pretend to, you understand, dear Milkee, and then I will give you the charm."

The proposition was not exactly to Milkeekokum's mind. "Still," thought he, "one's grandmother in a lion's skin cannot be such a terrible creature, especially when that grandmother is friendly disposed towards you," and so he made no objection.

"But where and how shall I meet you?" he asked.

"Take your spear and go out as for lion-hunting in the usual way," replied the wasp. "As for the rest, leave me to manage."

So saying, she rose on her wings and flew away, and in a few seconds the roar of a lion shook the forest-trees and Milkeekokum's house, and Milkeekokum too, for that matter, and he knew that she had changed her shape for the one that she liked best.

"She roars terribly strong for an old woman!" muttered he uneasily.

However, his hopes newly raised by the wasp's mysterious visit were too urgent to be daunted at trifles. "I'll venture it," said he—"I'll venture it at once, and it will be the sooner over." And skipping down his ladder, he commenced his preparations for a lion-hunting excursion.

They were very simple; all he needed was his spear, and an old kaross or cloak, and his palm-leaf hat, and then he set out, carefully bolting his street-door.

"It isn't as though it were earnest, it is a mere matter of form to satisfy the stupid old creature's whim," said he, and so screwing up his courage, he bent his steps in the direction whence the terrible roar had proceeded. It was some considerable time, however—near the evening, in fact—ere he discovered traces of the animal he was in search of; but at last his diligence was rewarded, and in the sand in the neighbourhood of some craggy and precipitous rocks he came on the creature's footmarks clearly defined.

Then he came to a standstill. There is but one recognised method of hunting the lion amongst the Hottentot nation, and that is to decoy the animal to a part of the rocks where one ledge rises abruptly above another. Then the hunter fastens his kaross and his cap on the top of his spear, and crouching at the lower ledge, elevates the dummy and waves it to and fro, so that the deluded lion above may mistake it for a man, and making a leap at it, miss his aim, and roll, with every bone within his valuable hide broken, to the bottom of the abyss. These were the tactics that Milkeekokum was bent on pursuing, and for that purpose, and as before mentioned, he had brought with him his cloak and his palm-leaf cap; but now he so nearly approached his game, he began to reflect whether that stupid old woman his grandmother knew enough about lion-hunting to justify her in commanding him to set out lion-hunting just in the ordinary way. "Because," mused Milkeekokum, " if she makes a leap at the dummy and throws a summerset down the precipice, she'll be killed to a certainty, and then I shall be no better off than ever! I know what I'll do; I'll hold up the lure, and just as she is going to spring I'll shout out and stop her!"

So he went a little farther, pausing to listen at every step, and presently he distinctly heard the sound of a large animal breathing hard, as though it was just dropping to sleep and would shortly begin to snore. As good fortune ordained, too, just at this spot the

rock shelved delightfully, and below was a fall of fifty feet, if an inch. The active young Kybob was not long in making his preparations. Hooking his kaross and cap to the end of his spear, he planted it firmly at the edge of the outer ledge, uttered a startling yell, and then bobbed down to await the result.

He had not long to wait. Instantly responding to his yell as mighty a roar as that Milkeekokum had at first heard rent the air, followed by a sound like the cracking of a waggon-whip, which the young man, who began to feel a curious sensation about the knee-joints, knew must be the lashing of the creature's tail. In another moment a hideous head, in which in vain Milkeekokum sought the image of his grandmother, peered over the edge of the top ledge, and then there was a whistling sound as of a lion cleaving the air, and for several seconds afterwards Milkeekokum lost all consciousness. The fact is, he was the victim of a rather extraordinary accident. He had fully made up his mind at the critical moment to warn the lion, for his grandmother's sake, that it had better not make the leap, but at once acknowledge itself subdued, but seeing it so little like his grandmother, and struck with the agonising thought that after all it might be the *wrong* lion, he grew suddenly confused, and when the animal leaped at the dummy the young man held so fast on at his end of the spear that he was carried sheer over the ledge along with the kaross and the lion, and, only that the latter being the heavier body reached the ground first, and Milkeekokum alighted plump on its soft, yielding flanks, he would infallibly have broken his neck. As it was, he merely rebounded a few feet high in the air, and alighted on his feet sound of wind and limb as ever.

So, too, did the lion, and that was the worst of it. It rose to its legs just as Milkeekokum gained his and had picked up his spear, evidently bereft of all power of utterance or motion by rage and astonishment. For a moment the young Kybob thought that he detected in the lion's left eye a cast of the same expression as that which distinguished his grandmother, but its visual orbits blazed so that he could not look long enough at them to make sure. "Anyhow, whether it be my grandmother or no," thought he, "it will be sure to come after me, and I may possibly find a more convenient spot for explanation than this is." And before the lion had recovered its presence of mind the young Kybob bounded away towards a grove of palms he could descry at a distance of about a mile and a quarter.

It was fortunate for him that he was a swift runner, for scarcely had he gained a hundred yards when the lion shook off the restraint that held him and came after Milkeekokum at a thundering rate. The young man heard it and turned an ear windward, hoping to hear himself called by name; but, to his dismay and confusion, he heard only the ordinary sounds that proceed from a beast of prey in danger of losing the game it is pursuing. This made him increase his speed; and while the lion was still a fair twenty yards in his rear, he reached the foremost of the grove of palms, and shying his spear up into its branches, swarmed up after it, active as a cat, just as his pursuer arrived at the bottom of the tree. For several seconds it paced about with open mouth and rageful eyes seeking a means of reaching the Hottentot, but finding it hopeless, it squatted down on its haunches and looked up with an expression of countenance that plainly enough intimated, "You haven't the best of the game yet, my friend."

Now Milkeekokum had a fair opportunity of examining the features of the beast intently, still hoping to discover that the inconvenience he had been put to arose out of his grandmother's jocular disposition than from any real threatening of danger. "Or perhaps she is a little huffed at being trapped over that precipice," thought Milkeekokum; "she will recover her good temper with her breath;" and so thinking he looked down, nodding, and winking, and endeavouring to conciliate his lionised relative by all manner of pleasant facial contortions.

But it was all of no use: the animal remained a grim, hungry lion with but one present purpose, a purpose that induced him to lick his lips from time to time and whet his talons against the tree bark. He called "Kaphoozlem" in as wheedling a tone as he could assume, but the lion only gaped wide in sickening hope and champed its terrible jaws. Really, however, this was Milkeekokum's translated grandmother—his grandmother but his bitter and implacable enemy, as the reader has doubtless by this time settled in his own mind. But she could not in that shape declare herself to the wicked young Kybob—it was out of her power. Although she might take the form of anything she pleased, it was only as a wasp that she was permitted the use of human features and language, which for the purposes of her revenge was a happy arrangement, otherwise she would in all probability have given Milkeekokum a piece of her mind as he crouched up in the tree making monkey faces at her, and so have put him on his guard, not that that would have saved him.

As the evening grew the lion became more impatient, walking round and about the tree whining and moaning, and evidently rapidly arriving at the melancholy conclusion that it were mere waste of time to stay any longer, and presently with a tremendous roar and a

Is it his Grandmother?

glance of deadliest hatred towards the young man, it betook itself to the depths of the forest with rapid strides.

Milkeekokum was in a quandary, and scarcely knew whether to be pleased or sorry that he was left to himself. After all, and although appearances were decidedly against the supposition, the creature that had just turned tail so discontentedly into the forest might have been his grandmother, in which case he should have got down and faced her, and even while he was turning the matter over in his troubled mind and listening for the lion's possible return, once more his ears were assailed by a humming sound of "s-s-s-p," and, settling on a leaf fairly under his nose, there once again was the wasp. It did not show its sting this time, it did not look angry in the least, but its tiny features were marked with an expression of sorrow and regret that was unmistakable.

"Hullo!" exclaimed Milkeekokum, not at all displeased under the circumstances to be face to face with his good old grandmother once more. "I am very glad to meet you once again, O Kaphoozlem. I have been in a terrible condition of mind since we last met."

The grandmother wasp shook her head sadly. "No condition of mind is more terrible than that of a coward when it is put to the test," she replied.

"Who says that Milkeekokum is a coward?" fiercely demanded the young warrior, involuntarily clenching his fist, and of a great mind to smash his grandmother on the spot.

"Ask the lion."

"Where would be the use, since it could not answer?" replied Milkeekokum cunningly. "I did not bargain to meet strange lions, but Kaphoozlem in shape of one. The one I met was a strange lion without doubt, since it could not reply when I spoke to it."

The wasp uttered a little laugh. "I was that lion," she said.

"Then why did you look so frightful?" asked the young Kybob; "why did you grind your teeth and champ your jaws at me? Why were you not sociable as you now are?"

"'Twas but to test my grandson's courage," said she. "Had you come down, as I dumbly invited you to" (here Milkeekokum shrugged his shoulders), "I should at once have declared myself, and by this time you would have known the delights of passing from one life to another. Now all the work remains to be done."

"Where is that lion now?" asked Milkeekokum after a few moments' reflection.

"Nowhere. I am the lion. Am I not a terrible creature to affright the nimblest young Kybob of his tribe?"

Milkeekokum felt his cheeks blushing a deep purple hue at the reproof conveyed in his grandmother's sarcasm.

"Make yourself into a lion again this instant," said he, grasping his spear, "and then see how I will serve you."

"Nay, that were no test," replied the wasp, "since you know that there is no danger. Your courage must be proved in some other way, my grandson, ere you will be deemed worthy to hold the great charm."

"Prove it how you will, I am ready," answered Milkeekokum desperately.

"It shall be proved this very night," said the wasp. "Promise me that you will chase and subdue and take fearlessly by the beard one of two creatures that shall cross your path before you get back to your hut."

"I promise," replied Milkeekokum readily.

"You will not let their shape fright you. Whatever form they—I, I mean, you know, dear Milkee—may take, you will face them manfully."

"I promise! I promise!" replied the young warrior impatiently.

"It is enough," said the wasp, and rising with a satisfied hum, she flew away.

Fully determined that there should be no mistake this time, Milkeekokum descended rapidly from the tree, and shouldering his spear, stepped out bravely, but not without a feeling of resentment against his grandmother. "The old idiot! as though she couldn't have given me the great charm without all this fuss! But I'll be quits with her. It is hard if a young warrior possessed of the charm is not stronger than a silly old woman with it. We'll play at lions then with a vengeance, I warrant."

Just as he had muttered this vindictive threat, with a loud fluttering voice a magnificent ostrich burst out of a thicket just to the right of him, and scudded away with all the speed of its long legs. Milkeekokum laughed. "O-oh!" said he, "is this one of the terrible creatures I am to hunt and take by the beard? What an old fool my grandmother is, to be sure!"

And he bounded after the ostrich, certain of getting over one half of his terrible task in a very easy manner. Nevertheless the ostrich was young and vigorous, and not easily overtaken. For several miles the chase continued, Milkeekokum growing more excited each moment. Once he came so close to the giant bird that he ventured to cast his spear at her, but of this he immediately repented, for it lodged amongst the magnificent plumage of her tail, and there remained, rather helping than hindering the great bird, since it spurred her to renewed exertion.

MILKEEKOKUM CONTINUES THE PURSUIT OF HIS GRANDMOTHER.

"Never mind," said Milkeekokum; "a hunter needs no spear in pursuing so wretched a creature as an ostrich; I will soon run it down and recover my weapon, and a prime bunch of feathers into the bargain."

Once more he put on a spurt of speed, and in half-an-hour or so was closer to his game than ever, when suddenly he heard a splash, and arrived at the brink of the river

THIS IS THE CLOSEST THAT MILKEEKOKUM EVER GOT TO THE "GREAT CHARM."

just in time to see the ostrich take a dive from the bank. Now Milkeekokum was indeed certain. He was even a better swimmer than runner. Without a moment's hesitation he plunged in.

"You can't keep your head under water very long, my beauty," chuckled he. "I shall have you by the beard before I could count up the number of my fingers and toes."

But he waited and waited, and the ostrich did not re-appear.

"Perhaps it has swung down the stream a little distance," said Milkeekokum. And he made a few strokes in that direction.

Suddenly, however, he heard a stirring of the water behind him, and hastily turned about, with his right hand open, ready, as he thought, to clutch the ostrich by the beard; but as he turned, a sight so appalling met his gaze that he leaped clean out of the water, excepting one foot. It was not the head of an ostrich that he beheld, but the wide-open and hideous maw of a hippopotamus! He would have cried out if the power had remained to him; but, as it was, sinking down into the water, with his head only above the surface of it, he could do nothing but gaze, horrified, into the monster's throat, the palate of which seemed to palpitate for his reception. He could not speak; he could not utter any sound; and amid the horrid stillness he suddenly heard for the third time that strange humming, and was conscious of the buzzing of little wings just over his head.

"O traitor to thy tribe! poisoner of thy kindred!" cried a little voice, "see now to what horrible depths thy ambition has led thee! Tremble, O Milkeekokum, for the new life thou shalt presently awake to!"

That was the last of it. Simultaneously with the flitting off of the wasp was heard a crashing together of mighty jaws, and Milkeekokum had vanished.

THE LUCKLESS ADDAPHANG.

THE LUCKLESS ADDAPHANG.

PYNCHBLOO, SKRAPESHYN, AND LUPE AT THEIR BARBAROUS SUPPER.

It is not generally known that the true reason why the Patagonians have ceased to be giants, and have dwindled down to the stature of ordinary men, is that during the last century and a-half, or perhaps rather more, they have set their hearts against the consumption of seal's flesh, which previous to the time in question formed the staple of their diet. To this day all the research and experiments of the profoundest philosophers have failed to discover in what part of the seal this wonderful virtue lay, some opining that it is concealed in the fat that is found between the skin and the flesh, others ascribing it to the marrow, while not a few persist in declaring that the fish is equally virtuous from his snout to his tail's tip, and that the grand secret rests in the mode of cooking it. The best proof, however, that none of them are a bit nearer the truth than when they started is to be found in the fact that, despite their practical inquiries, not a man amongst them is taller by an atom of an inch.

It is scarcely surprising, since they are so completely in the dark as to the manner in which the seal assisted the Patagonian in his growth, that they should be equally ignorant of the reason why the natives abandoned the eating of it. It is the less surprising when it is known that the story involving the reason is one which is never more than whispered, and that amongst old and discreet folk who would not be likely to spread it abroad. How it came to my knowledge I may not reveal. Sometimes of blusterous nights I walk out with a sealskin cap on my head, with lappets to keep my ears warm; perhaps the wind stirring the fur of the lappets awoke some sort of witchery there lying dormant, and the witch and the wind together let me into the secret. I do not say that it happened so: I merely suggest that it might.

It is the more likely because if there is a country more than another plagued by witches it is Patagonia. You can never get away from them. The very dog lying on the hearth may be a witch in disguise, the water bubbling in the clay pot on the fire may contain three or four witches—for they have the power to translate themselves into the tiniest shapes—the stick you thrust under the pot to make it boil may conceal a witch that will for the rest of your life cherish against you the deadliest spite for burning her; your wife—if you are a Patagonian—may be a witch, and if you have three daughters, if not more than one has private dealings with the Evil One you may congratulate yourself as lucky.

There was once a Patagonian, Krowfyshook by name, and he had four daughters, and they all were witches. How it came about the afflicted father knew no more than you or I, any further than that their great-grandmother was known to be a witch, and might have changed them in the cradle. The father knew that they were witches, not from any hideousness or deformity afflicting them, but on account of their marvellous beauty. Even while they were yet sucklings their hair stuck out in a fierce bush to the extent of a foot at least, and the nails on their fingers and toes were long and crooked as the claws of a bird, and their spreading ears served as a boundary to the majestic breadth of their chubby-lipped mouths.

And so they grew in loveliness, Krowfyshook more and more convinced of their witchery, but carefully concealing the conviction even from his most intimate friend, not for fear that harm might fall on his daughters—for however a witch may be hated there are none who will lay a finger on her to harm her—but in dread lest he might be put to death as being responsible for their coming into the world. Besides, they did not hurt him; indeed, although he never acknowledged it, he had shrewd suspicions that they had by their magic done him at least one most excellent service. Their mother was grown old and ugly, and at times made Krowfyshook's hut unhappy by her jealous outbursts. One day in a passion she struck her youngest daughter Addaphang, but that dutiful child did not return the blow; she merely hurried out of the hut shaking her fist at her parent, as an intimation that the outrage would not be forgotten. Shortly after the mother went out too, to fetch a skin of water from the river, and somehow or other she slipped in and was drowned. Krowfyshook said nothing, but as young Addaphang crouched by the fire that evening he observed that her hair steamed as though it had recently been made very wet and was now drying, and with a grateful sigh he helped her to a liberal slice of the smoked dog's flesh off which the family was supping.

There was Addaphang, and Pynchbloo, and Skrapeshyn, and Lupe, and of the four when they came to woman's estate it was hard to say which was the loveliest. Nobody but their father in the least suspected their diabolical power, and all the single young men of the island were madly, frantically in love with them. The chief, Swyvlgoggle, was not a single man, indeed, the number of wives he at present possessed was quite disgraceful, nevertheless he cast eyes at the sisters—at all four of them—and it was only because he could not make up his mind which was the most charming that he did not make an offer.

Like all witches they hated each other cordially. If there was a pin to choose amongst them, Addaphang was the best, and on that account the other three agreed to hate her with all the power of vindictive partnership. The chief reason why they hated her, however, was that her hair was more than theirs inclined to red, and red hair was known to be Swyvlgoggle's admiration, and more than once when the sisters were in company, the chief had been known to regard Addaphang in a manner that they could not help remarking.

But there was another circumstance that, had Addaphang's sisters known it, would have increased their animosity against her a hundredfold. She loved Swyvlgoggle— loved him passionately and deliriously. Whenever she could escape the jealous and watchful eyes of her sisters she was off and away to be in the mighty chief's delightful society. Not in her own proper shape, that would have been too scandalous. No; she would take the form of a fly and sit on his shoulder and listen to his conversation, and if it pleased her she would even venture to alight on his cheeks and snatch a kiss from his sweet mouth. On one such occasion when he had excited her gratitude by making mention of her, and she had essayed to kiss him for it, at the identical moment he drew such a powerful breath towards a sigh as nearly drew her down his throat. After that she was more careful.

But time flew by and still Swyvlgoggle made no proposition, indeed, his love seemed changing from her to Pynchbloo, who, although her hair was not red but dark as cinders, had a charming cast in her right eye that almost made amends; and the more despondent Addaphang grew the more her malicious sisters derided her and called her bad names, and set on her, and beat her, so that she was often glad to assume her favourite shape of a fly to get away. At last matters arrived at such a pass that she resolved to take measures for her own protection and to secure Swyvlgoggle all to herself; not perhaps in the way she would most have desired, but she was so bebadgered and worried, poor thing, as to be glad to avail herself of the first likely expedient that entered into her head.

Of all sports by land or sea, there was none in which Swyvlgoggle took so much delight as in seal-catching. He liked the sport, and he liked the flesh of his game; and very frequently in the season he would absent himself from home during several days and nights, to return from his solitary excursion tired and weary, but sleek and happy, and two stone heavier.

It was her knowledge of what was the chief's favourite sport that suggested the novel scheme to Addaphang. "There are many ways of existing that present fewer inducements than that of the seal," said she. "It must be delightfully cool down in the still blue water, and nicer than anything I have met in my hateful woman shape, to lie along the soft sand and doze in the sun. I'll be a seal for the future—a seal happy and fat. Swyvlgoggle shall go towards fattening me. I know that it is not in the nature of the common seal to eat mankind, but I will be an uncommon seal. I'll change myself into

THE LUCKLESS ADDAPHANG. 49

that animal's shape and cast myself in the way of my dear, dear Swyvlgoggle, and make a meal of him, and content myself to live in the peaceful waters away from my spiteful sisters ever afterwards."

So that very evening she slipped away from her sisters, and betaking herself as a fly to Swyvlgoggle, and perching on his hair, heard him bid his chief wife make him a good-

THIS IS HOW SWYVLGOGGLE WAS LURED TO DESTRUCTION.

sized parcel of cold meat and bread, as early next morning he was off to the banks of the Brineigh to hunt for seals, and might be gone some days. This was enough for Addaphang; she immediately made up her mind to return home no more, but to repair at once to the Brineigh, which was distant about eleven and a-half leagues. This determination sealed her fate, since it is a law amongst Patagonian witches that if they assume a second shape without first returning to their original and proper one, the said second shape shall be the one they shall wear for a hundred years, when they are free to retake human form if so inclined.

And so it came about that about noon of the day following that on which he set out, Swyvlgoggle wandering on the banks of the Brineigh, club in hand ready for his game, he spied the loveliest seal it was ever his good luck to clap eyes on, and sound asleep as a roach. It lay very near the water, and for fear that it should escape, Swyvlgoggle stepped with the lightness of a cat to where the splendid creature lay. Careful as were his movements, however, the seal was disturbed by them, and moved, in a sleepy manner, towards the water, which, although the chief quickened his movements, it gained ere he could reach it. So splendid a prize, however, was not to slip so easily through the fingers of Swyvlgoggle. With a cry and a tremendous leap he is in the water too; and had the seal been of ordinary nature, it had little time to live; but alas! under the peculiar circumstances, the tables were turned; with a backward spring the witch-seal faced the affrighted huntsman, and clasping him round the neck in its flippers, sank like a stone with him to the depths of the Brineigh.

And never would the appalling fate of Swyvlgoggle have been suspected but for the jealous watching and prying of Addaphang's sister Pynchbloo. Finding that she did not return to the paternal hut all night, Pynchbloo's worst fears were aroused, and she set out to look for her in shape of a dog. Her first visit was to Swyvlgoggle's camp, and there, prowling amongst the warriors, she learned that the chief was away seal-hunting, no one knew where. This was enough for the jealous witch. "That is all a pretence," said she to herself, finding great relief for her rage in gnawing a bullock-bone at that moment thrown aside from the dinner. "He has eloped with that forward hussy, and I'll find 'em, if I run my legs off."

Having a dog's shape, she was likewise endowed with the scent of one, and running in a circle, she presently struck on Swyvlgoggle's trail, and, with her nose to the ground, sedulously followed it. For miles and miles she trotted on, her rage increasing as the scent grew stronger, until she reached the shore of the Brineigh. Just too late, however. From a distance she heard the cry that Swyvlgoggle gave as he plunged into the lake, and she saw likewise a head not his rise suddenly and then disappear, and though she raced like a mad dog down to the strand, she saw no more.

For a long while she remained staring at the water in furious bewilderment, for all the world as though she were suffering under an attack of hydrophobia. That her sister

Addaphang was concerned in the mystery she had no manner of doubt. Hers was the strange head that had for a moment appeared above the surface, but beyond that it was the head of a fish the distance at which she saw it was too great to enable her to pronounce. What was to be done? For a time she had a great mind to change into a fish, and dive in and investigate the business, but to do so without first returning home and assuming her woman's shape would be to merit the penalty already mentioned. So she thought better of it, and fast as her legs would carry her she galloped home, and told her sisters what she had seen.

Their rage and consternation was as great as hers, and the three laid their wicked heads together. Lupe, the eldest, was likewise the most cunning. "If she lured him to eat him," said she, "she will be too full and lazy to travel far from the spot where you saw her sink. Let us make an outcry at once, and declare that we saw the chief dragged in by a great fish, and set them to work dragging for it that they may secure the iron ring of chieftainship that Swyvlgoggle wore about his wrist, and without which no other chief can be elected. We shall know if the fish they catch is our hateful sister, because, as you know, whatever shape she takes she cannot alter her eyes, and those I could swear to out of ten thousand."

"So could I," cried Skrapeshyn.

"And I," said Pynchbloo.

So they ran out and made an outcry, and told what they had seen, and for the sake of rescuing the precious ring a gang of fishermen at once set out, and, guided by the sisters, speedily reached the spot where Swyvlgoggle was last seen, and there they baited their hooks, the mob keeping a long distance away, for fear that the monster fish might grow alarmed at their noise, and escape farther out into the lake.

And they fished and they fished all night, and towards morning they felt a tremendous tug at their lines, and hauling in brought up the most gigantic porpoise ever caught in those waters, and triumphantly shouldering it they carried it to where the sisters and the mob were waiting, crying "We have captured it! We have caught the ravenous monster that swallowed our Swyvlgoggle!" And observing the extraordinary size of the porpoise, the witch sisters really thought that the fishermen had had good luck with the last cast, but when they came near enough with their load Pynchbloo slily applied her thumb to the eyelid of the dead fish, and, from the manner of biting her nether lip and the glance of rage and disappointment she shot at Lupe and Skrapeshyn, they were at once convinced of their error.

But they said nothing, and the fishermen had to find out for themselves that the fish they had taken was not the one that had swallowed their chief. While they were hacking the porpoise with their knives, and before they had cut down to the part in which they expected to discover relics of Swyvlgoggle, a little boy picked up a piece of the fish, and was about to swallow it, when, with a scream of terror, his mother seized him by the throat and compelled him to disgorge it. "Ah, little wretch!" said she, "would you eat of the cursed fish that has cropped off the flourishing head of our tribe? Would you take into your hungry little belly the porpoise-poison that in future must be banished with loathing from amongst us?" When the witch sisters heard this they glanced at each other meaningly and shrugged their shoulders.

But the porpoise was sliced to mincemeat, and nothing of Swyvlgoggle discovered in its interior, not even the iron ring of office they were so anxious to retain possession of. They were terribly disappointed, but there was no help for it.

"We will go home and rest," said the fisherman. (They had been out all night, be it remembered.) "We will go home and rest, and to-morrow we will come and try our luck again."

"The sort of luck they will have is bespoke, then," grumbled Lupe. "By to-morrow the monster, whatever it is, will have rested too after its horrible meal, and will be off miles and miles down the Brineigh."

She said this in a low voice, and as though it were intended for her sister Pynchbloo's hearing; but, as she expected, the people about caught the observation, and began to complain against the fishermen for their lack of spirit.

"It is all very well for you who have had nothing to do but to sit or lie about all through the night," spoke the blunt foreman of the fishers; "but with us, who have been watching and hauling since sundown, it is a different matter. What better can we do than we have done? If we knew the identical spot where Pynchbloo saw our noble Swyvlgoggle vanish, we might have a better chance."

"I could find the spot in an instant," spoke Pynchbloo hurriedly; and so she could, and that by a token unmistakable. As has already been stated, when in the shape of a dog she had behaved as one, and in her despairing rage tore up the sand with her feet until quite a deep hole was made, with a heap by the side of it. "I can take you straight to the spot within a foot, good fishermen," said Pynchbloo. "Come at once, and I will come too, and help carry your spears."

Such an appeal it was impossible to resist. Had an ordinary woman spoken it might have been different, but Pynchbloo was the pride and beauty of her tribe, and as she uttered the encouraging words there was a fire in her eyes, especially in the one that was a little askew, that the simple fishermen mistook for chivalry, though in fact it was merely consuming hatred for poor Addaphang, her sister. So with one voice they bade her lead on, and they would follow.

Straight she led them to the spot where the scratched-up heap was, and there they cast in their bait. There were seven hooks hung within a circle of a yard—Pynchbloo was so certain of the exact spot—and the centre hook the witch baited herself, weaving a charm with the bait that no fish could possibly resist. Then they all sat down on the beach to watch for a bite.

They waited so long that the sleepy fishermen began to yawn and gape, when all of a sudden there was a tug at the lines of so violent a nature that the water leaped up with a sounding splash and awoke the fishermen. It was the centre hook of the seven that had took, and grasping that line all together with a will hauled in, Pynchbloo encouraging them by voice and gesture. So immense was the weight at the other end of the line, however, and so prodigious the struggles of the creature attached to it, that for all their exertions they made no way at all, and were obliged to beckon to the mob for help, whereon a dwarf, scarcely six feet high, but stronger than a horse, came and added his hauling power to the other. Then the great fish yielded. Its struggles became fainter and fainter, while Pynchbloo stood craning her neck at the water's brink, trembling with anxiety to see the sort of fish that would presently make its appearance.

And her malicious longing was gratified. In a little while the blunt brown nose of a seal appeared above the surface, and in an instant a pair of eyes which were not seal's eyes but human. To hear the scream of diabolical joy that Pynchbloo uttered, to see her dance and clap her skinny hands, was the finest delight her two wicked sisters had ever experienced. But how was it with her third sister, the luckless Addaphang, who all for love of her sweetheart had eaten him, and who now had been treacherously betrayed up out of the hole in the rock, where she was lying so peaceful and contented, by the potent spells of Pynchbloo? The eyes of the seal sister and the other met, and had not the latter possessed a heart of stone she surely would have relented before that imploring, appealing gaze. But she was inexorable, and only danced and screamed with more energy, calling on the fishermen and begging them to hold tight and drag away their hardest, as now, without doubt, they had caught the monster that had devoured Swyvlgoggle. And when poor Addaphang saw how matters stood and how little mercy she might expect at the hands of her sisters, she resisted with all her might, and backed water with her flippers and endeavoured to get the line between her teeth that she might bite it in two. But it was all of no use. With her poor mouth dreadfully excoriated, and exhausted and faint, she was dragged up on to the beach and there was butchered before the eyes of her sisters. There could be no doubt as to her guilt, for the precious ring was there to prove it.

So from that very hour the Patagonians cursed the seal and would eat no more of its flesh, because that the blood of Chief Swyvlgoggle was on its head, and ever since they have dwindled and become littler and littler. Whether the spirit of the witch Addaphang has aught to do with this dwindling is hard to say. According to Patagonian testimony this is impossible. Had her seal remains been allowed to abide until they decayed in the hole where the enraged people threw them, she might have come to life again in a hundred years; but the sisters were too cunning and too inveterate against her to give her this chance. That very night, when the village was wrapped in slumber, they stole away together to where the seal's body was thrown, and collected it, and made a fire behind a rock, and roasted it and eat it up to the very last mouthful.

I have tried, but in vain, to discover what became of Pynchbloo, Skrapeshyn, and Lupe after this diabolical and cannibal act. It is as well, perhaps, for without doubt the account would prove too terrible to print.

THE ELK DEMON.

The Elk Demon receives his Coup-de-Grâce.

THE ELK DEMON.

EXACTLY one hundred years ago, the country on the western shore of the Great Yellow Stone—which, as everybody at all acquainted with North American Indian history is aware, was at that time the dwelling-place of that brave and renowned tribe the Randans —was sorely afflicted.

It was not war that was desolating the land. The Kickshaws, who dwelt on the opposite side of the river, were the nearest people who by number and skill in arms could pretend to face the terrible Randans, and they had remained quiet during the long period of nine months, a circumstance sufficiently explained by the fact that nine hundred and forty Kickshaw scalps taken in the last battle adorned the inner canvas of the great wigwam of the Randans. It was not drought that was scourging the country; never had rain fallen in greater abundance, never had there been lovelier weather for the growth of grass and corn. The calamity did not take the familiar shape of small-pox amongst the tribe, for excepting the very small children every soul in the colony had passed through that terrible ordeal, as the prevalence of scarred visages attested. No, it was none of these evils that afflicted the Randans—it was famine.

Yes, as before stated, it was spring time, and the rain fell abundantly, and everything was favourable to the growth of corn wherewith to make bread, and of grass to feed the cattle. Nay, the grass and the corn *did* grow, and herein lay the mystery that filled men's breasts with awe and amazement. In those patches where the corn was sown come early morning there it might be seen thrusting its thousand tiny heads through the red earth, green and vigorous, and showing signs of a bountiful and speedy crop, and during the day, encouraged by the sun's comforting heat, it continued to sprout and increase in height famously. Then the Randans would take heart, and whisper to each other, "It has all come right at last; the witchcraft is taken off our corn, and in three weeks it will be of full growth, and in a week beyond that ripe enough for harvesting; then will there be an end to our alarms, and with so fair a prospect may we freely consume our store of last year's growth." But alas! the comforting assurance that lulled them to sleep was dispelled with the next sunrise like dew from off the plains, for when they hastened to the patches where yesterday the grain was growing so promisingly, to their unspeakable dismay they discovered that instead of being at least as tall again as when they last beheld it, it had dwindled and grown *shorter*, so that no more than of the length of a man's thumb-nail was to be seen above the surface, and that blunt and stunted, as though a tremendous reaping-knife with a jagged edge had swept over it, sawing it close off to the earth.

It was the same with the grass and with every green thing that grew, and though, as before stated, it was the most fruitful season of the whole year, scarce had such distress been known amongst the Randans in the severest winter. Luckily they were not of that thriftless hand-to-mouth order of savages such as are to be commonly met with in these regions. As yet there remained in store some considerable quantity of parched corn and buffalo-berries, besides some *pemican*, which, as the reader is doubtless aware, is the Indian name for buffalo-meat dried in the sun till it attains the colour and hardness of mahogany, in which state it is pounded to dust, and, being mixed with water, is baked into very palatable cakes. Very much more of the commodities might have been stored, but hitherto it had been found necessary to provide against the "ice months" only, and it was only when matters began to assume so sinister a complexion that the rulers of the tribe began to think seriously of husbanding their remaining resources, dealing out limited rations to each family.

Nor was this the worst part of it. Though preferring bread with their meat, animal food alone would not for a time have been seriously objected to, and at ordinary seasons there would have been no stint of it, for when the young herbage is cropping up it is a rare time for deer, and the poor pinched-up anatomies who have found it hard work to crawl through the winter plump up in a wonderful way, and grow so fat and unwieldy that half-an-hour's chase on horseback is sufficient to run down the fleetest of the flock. But now there was nothing for the deer to eat, and they remained with all their winter gauntness and swift as greyhounds. There was no chance of catching one except by means of the pitfall, for the horses, like the deer, suffered from want of provender, and were weak, and thin, and hungry, being often glad to make a supper off the hide thong that tethered them to the post.

How to explain the mystery no one knew. The chief medicine-man was consulted, and though he had no hesitation in declaring that the marvellous failure in the crops was the result of witchcraft, he was as much puzzled as anybody to tell the manner of witch that was working the dire mischief, or where it sprang from, or how it might be laid. There were three old women of the Kickshaw nation taken in the last battle, and kept alive to do drudgery out of compassion for their grey heads, the hairs on which were so few as to preclude the possibility of taking a scalp from them, and the Grand Medicine, after considering the matter, thought it not improbable that the witch might originate in one or other of the unlucky trio, and in the midst of a great circle formed of the whole number of the tribe assembled they were duly roasted alive, and their ashes scattered to the winds. Come the following morning, however, it was plain that the suspicions of Grand Medicine were unfounded, for there were the green blades gnawed close to the earth as before.

Next it came into the head of Grand Medicine that perhaps the gods were angry with them for laying up a store of parched corn and buffalo-berries, instead of placing implicit reliance in their power to provide for the people in their need, and suggested that a burnt sacrifice of one-half of the edibles in stock should be made by way of convincing the gods of the perfect faith of the tribe. This suggestion, like the preceding one, was promptly adopted, with no better result than that next morning the growing crops were as stumpy as ever and their larder provokingly impoverished.

The next step was for the people to grow furious against their Grand Medicine for advising them so rashly, and as a penalty to set him up as a target for their tomahawks until he was hacked all to little bits: still the corn and the grass grew no better than before.

Every day matters grew more and more serious. Had they resolved on such a course when the mysterious calamity first befell them, nothing would have been easier than to have crossed the Yellow Stone river and helped themselves out of the abundance of the Kickshaws, whose crops, as might be plainly seen from the hill-tops, were fruitful as could be desired. But now it was altogether too late for such an expedient; the warriors of the tribe were weakened by long fasting, and in no condition to provoke a quarrel with a neighbour, who even as the matter stood had a long score against them. Besides, it was of the utmost importance that their famished condition should be kept from the knowledge of the Kickshaws, who somehow had got wind of the story of the three old women, and were, so spies reported, only restrained from paying a vengeful visit in their canoe fleet to the Randan shore by the memory of what tremendous fellows their enemies had shown themselves when they last came to blows. So, in order that the Kickshaws might have no suspicion of the terrible straits to which the Randans were reduced, a picked crew of the latter were selected and carefully fattened out of the dwindling larder, their duty being to proceed daily in their various canoes and paddle within a little distance of the Kickshaw strand at different points, not ostentatiously, but in a free and easy manner, so as to show themselves as specimens of the sort of fellows they (the Kickshaws) would have to deal with in case they were rash enough to cut up rough consequent upon that little affair of the three old women.

But behind all this pretence and masking, the face of the Randan nation was rapidly growing hollow-eyed and bony. Day by day and week by week flew by, until the spring became summer and summer autumn, and the stunted and still mysteriously gnawed-off corn-stalks ripened and turned yellow, and the equally mysteriously gnawed-off grass-blades sprouted nothing but blunt hay stubble. Now indeed were the prospects of the tribe dismal! For many weeks every man, woman, and child of it had subsisted on deer and bear flesh, and very little and lean of that, for, as before remarked, being in a condition of semi-starvation, those animals were exceedingly light and active, and at least a fair match as to speed with the Randan horses, who were kept alive on the green reeds and bulrushes that grew neglected on the opposite side of the river, and which were cut and stolen in the night by the more adventurous ones of the stricken tribe.

Different indeed were the ways of the people compared with what they were in prosperous times. Then, the labours of the day at an end, the squaws and the children would retire to their tents, while the men gathered in a social circle by the light of the fair moon, or, if the evenings were chilly, by the light of the pine-wood fire, and smoked their pipes, and sang their songs, and told stories of love and heroism, and the sounds of their mirth might have been heard by the envious Kickshaws on the other side of the mile-wide river. Now all this was altered. For fear of the invisible horror that was plaguing them they dare not stir out after nightfall, and though the evenings were balmy and the sky serene and inviting, soon as dusk fell they retired and shut themselves in—the men in the men's camps and the women in the women's camps—and cowered over their fires, and whispered tales of magic and witchcraft until the hair on their heads might have been heard to rise and to rustle, because of their trembling, like shaken straw. Even the great tent—that which was distinguished by the eagle's wings and the golden arrow crowning its summit, the tent of the mighty Chypchancy, chief of the tribe—was no exception to this melancholy rule. No one but the bravest of the brave, grisly warriors who had plucked laurels by the score from their enemies' heads, and young men of promise, were there admitted. Young indeed were some of these, striplings of scarcely six feet, and with the soft down of boyhood yet gracing their chins, but a glance at their wampum belts would discover nine scalps at least there suspended, that being the smallest number on which a young brave might found his pretension to admission to the great council house. Most conspicuous amongst these youthful braves was young Pitchanicker.

Pitchanicker carried thirteen scalps at his belt, and his bearing was proud, as well it might be, considering the noble stock from which he sprang. The renowned Knofunkyn was his grandfather, and the famous Nuckledown his father—Nuckledown, who, at the time the Randans were at deadly war with the Leepfrogs, disguised himself as one of the enemy, and making his way to the hostile camp there sought and gained admittance, and availed himself of the hospitality of the Leepfrog chief, until, a fitting opportunity presenting itself, he poisoned him and his entire family and brought away his scalp in triumph. Nor was it on this achievement alone that Nuckledown's fame was founded. Some time after the affair above related, the valiant Randan, made over-bold by his great success, once more penetrated to the Leepfrog country in furtherance of a design the details of which, although he admitted that they were ten times more diabolical than any one could possibly imagine, he declined to disclose; they were to wait and see, was his answer to all questions on the subject. They did wait, but they never saw. The mission miscarried: the gallant brave was discovered and captured, and doomed to death by torture. But did his proud spirit then relent? Did he abate one jot of his deadly spite against the enemies of his tribe? Listen. The sentence on Nuckledown was that he should be tethered to a pole and lashed to death with thongs of deerhide, steeped in fat and set alight, the squaws of the Leepfrogs being his executioners. So they tied him, giving him plenty of rope so that he might run wide and make good sport, and the women lit their thongs and began to lash him. And did Nuckledown flinch? Not he. He bore the stripes with an affected look of amused amazement, and then he broke into a loud laugh, and laughed the louder the harder the squaws laid on. "Is this how the Leepfrogs torture their enemies?" he cried; "do they tickle them till they laugh their lives out? Nay, pray let me die a death more becoming a warrior. Be as kind to me at least as we were to your brave Tuppinituckin, whom we captured, and give me a warm cloak." Now, although the Leepfrogs knew that the pride of their army, Tuppinituckin, had fallen into the hands of the Randans and by them been tortured to death, they were ignorant of the manner of the performance, and now eagerly demanded of Nuckledown what he meant by a warm cloak. He told them. They got the hide of a fat buck, and further anointed it with grease, and they had set fire to it and rolled Tuppinituckin in it. That was the "warm cloak," and though the Leepfrogs, when they heard the explanation, which Nuckledown gave in his drollest manner and as though it were the funniest job he had ever assisted at, were ready to tear him limb from limb, they could not in their hearts but acknowledge how very superior in ingenuity the Randans were to themselves, and they at once resolved to accept a leaf out of their book and apply it to the present case. Quickly the hide of a fat buck was procured and prepared according to Nuckledown's directions, who ordered the matter as coolly as though the buck that provided the terrible cloak was about to be roasted for his dinner. When all was in readiness, the young chief, who succeeded his father whom Nuckledown had poisoned, stepped forward holding the flaming cloak by its edges in readiness to cast it over Nuckledown's shoulders, but that wily brave, just in the nick of time, caught the young chief in his arms, and flinging himself to the ground, by a dexterous wriggle enveloped both himself and the young man within the hide's fiery folds, and so they perished together. Which was a very shocking business and one which I am very unwilling to bring under the notice of the reader, who possibly may be frightened into fits by it; indeed, not one word concerning Nuckledown should have here appeared, only that when his son was found performing such unheard-of deeds of valour and bravery, the question would naturally arise, what sort of a man could his father have been? Now, however, as the matter is adjusted, the reader will be spared this trouble.

Worthy of such a father did Pitchanicker appear as he sat that evening with the rest in the great council-tent. As was the case with all the rest, Famine had set her brand on his face, and his cheeks were pinched, and his eyes cavernous, and the fire in them, glowing in such deep shade, was terrible to behold. He sat in a gloomy part of the council-tent, so that the light of the pine-wood fire did not rest on any part of him; his arms were folded tightly across his bosom, and as his fierce eyes peered from under his bent brows, gazing fixedly at some object close to where the grave chief Chypchaney reclined, his breast heaved, and the nervous play of his thin lips from time to time revealed his closely-set teeth.

What was the object that Pitchanicker gazed at so intently? It has been said that all assembled in the council-tent were equally famine-stricken in appearance, but there was an exception. This was an old man of distinction evidently, for he wore the sacred vestments of Grand Medicine—the untanned yellow bearskin, trimmed with the dried skins of toads and snakes, and the necklace of teeth, claws, and talons of wild beasts—the vestments, indeed, of the late unlucky medicine-man, whose blundering advice as to the wasteful sacrifice had cost him his life. By his side hung his medicine-drum, and instead of scalps at his girdle, there hung innocent little charms and philtres for the curing of every disease under the sun. What, however, was more remarkable about him than anything else was that whereas every one about him was lank as crows in winter, this man was plump and sleek-looking as a pig fatted for killing. He was long-bellied like a pig, and as he squatted on the ground the easy arch of his back was suggestive of the same quadruped under prosperous circumstances; but at his shoulders the porcine likeness failed, and he became like another animal.

Why, is difficult to say, since he had neither antlers nor hair of any kind upon his face, but it was impossible to look on him without being reminded of a creature of the stag tribe. His face was not long like a stag's, but, on the contrary, round and double-chinned; his forehead was not square like a stag's, but oval and shooting straight up from his eyes to the crown of his head. It was his eyes that made him like a stag; they were full, brown, restless eyes, set in rigid-looking orbits, but shifting hither and thither with a rapidity and wide-awakedness peculiar to the suspicious animal he reminded one of. He was not a Randan by birth, but had been adopted into the tribe when a boy, and the circumstances attending his adoption were somewhat singular.

At the time in question the Omiaye nation, once the strongest and most powerful in Northern America, were through disease and a long series of disastrous wars reduced to such miserable straits as to be glad to sell their territory piecemeal to neighbouring tribes for just as little or much as they chose to give for it. The Randans, then growing into power, owned land adjoining that of the Omiayes, and from time to time on easy terms increased their possessions at the expense of the unfortunate ones. There was one property, however, which had remained with the Omiayes from time immemorial and which they still stuck to, declining to sell or barter it in any shape or way; nor could other be expected, since it was from this very possession that they drew their distinction and fame amongst surrounding nations. It was not much to look at, this said property; indeed, unless you were in the secret you would have passed it with no more concern than though it were a bit of useless and dirty rock springing up out of the ground. So it was a piece of rock, but not useless by a long way, for it was composed of the true and sacred pipe-stone, and from it were carved the bowls of every calumet ever smoked at a war-breeding or a peace-treaty throughout the land.   There was no other such rock in North America, so the Omiayes did all the sacred pipe-bowl trade, and as the price they charged for a piece of any size was about equal to ten times its weight in gold, it was without doubt a possession worth prizing and jealously guarding.   Besides, there was a view to be taken of it superior to the mercenary view.   It was only fair to infer that the spot where the gods planted the sacred pipe-stone would always be looked on with a kindly eye, and though the late experiences of the unlucky Omiayes were calculated to shake their faith, they clung to the old belief, and they struggled on, hoping for better times.

The Randans were extremely covetous after this pipe-stone rock. They had no idea of settling down in the Omiaye country, and setting up as guardians of the sacred thing; they thought that a better and more profitable measure would be to dig away a good-sized block of it and carry it off, at the same time destroying all that was left. After all, the demand for sacred pipe-stone was not large, and if the commodity were thus made scarce, it might be retailed at at least treble the old price, so that its possessors would be as well off as though they possessed the whole rock.

As before stated, however, the Omiayes, reduced though they were to the direst depths of poverty, would not hear of parting with their precious treasure; so since the Randans were bent on having it, there was nothing left for them but to take it by force, and this they proceeded to do with that earnestness that so invariably distinguished them on such occasions. Seeking a fair opportunity—it was in the dead of winter, and small-pox was ravaging the tents of the Omiayes from one end of the village to the other—the Randans fell on them in the night, clubbing and tomahawking all they met, whether they resisted or no.   By this means they cleared a speedy way to the spot where the pipe-stone rock was guarded by the Grand Medicine of the tribe, who with his little grandson lived in a hut just in front of it, so that to get at the pipe-stone rock it was necessary to pass through the hut of the Grand Medicine. But the stanch old savage was true to his post, and barred the way, threatening death to any who should dare invade what he called the temple of the sacred pipe-stone; but the mighty Randans had not advanced so far to be baffled and turned back by an old man, and finding that to force the hut would lead to the sacrifice of at least one life, a Randan brave more intrepid than his fellows presently threw a torch up on to the thatch of the rock-keeper's house, and speedily the place was in a blaze.

THE ELK DEMON. 71

But the spirit of a true Omiaye stirred the breast of the old Indian. Catching his little grandson up in his arms, he covered him with his blanket, so that he might be protected from the encroaching fire, and as the walls of his house fell, and he got a view of the mob of yelling and exultant braves, thus he spoke to them:—

"Dogs of Randans, and worse than dogs, wait but a little and ye shall find how this your great sin shall turn and sting you. What ye covet ye can never have; so yourselves ordained when ye fired my hut. Since ye have come, however, ye shall not go away empty-handed. Take ye this child, and with him my curse. Slay him if thou wilt. I beg you to slay him instantly, that his totem may be free to devour you, as it shall, as it shall."

And so saying, with supernatural strength he threw the child through the gathering flames far out to them, and just as he did so a tremendous bang was heard which extinguished the fire in the hut and made all dark in a moment, while a great cloud of dust arose as it were out of its ruins; and when, not heeding the old man's prophetic words, nor the strange explosion which followed, they rushed with mad yells to the spot where the sacred pipe-stone rock but just now was, they found it blackened and blown to ashes, so that not one piece big enough to make a single pipe-head could be discovered, though there and then by torch-light they dug down to a depth of several feet.

Now, had the Randans been as wise as their neighbours the Omiayes, they would have regarded themselves as simply outwitted in this business, and made the best of a bad job. Had they been as wise as the Omiayes, they would have known of the existence of gunpowder, and of what a very useful agent it is in destroying any coveted thing, such as a pipe-stone rock for instance, when you can no longer hold it, and the enemy is congratulating himself on having it all but in his hands. But the Randans had not as yet heard about gunpowder, and when they found that all in an instant rock and rock-keeper had vanished, leaving nothing but rubbish behind, they began to experience uncomfortable qualms, and to reflect that perhaps they had gone a little too far in meddling with matters sacred and mysterious, and if they could have been allowed would willingly have repaired the damage they had caused. As it was, there was nothing to be done but to hunt up and knock on the head every Omiaye they could discover, as the surest means of keeping the particulars of the affair amongst themselves, and then to make their way quietly to their own village.

It was while hunting about for the enemy that they came upon the child the old rock-minder had thrown out of the burning hut. As he had fallen so he lay, stunned and motionless. They had been much too eager to get at the pipe-stone rock to think about the child or what the old Omiaye had said respecting him to trouble themselves concerning him; but now that they came upon him after the sacred rock had vanished in a manner so inexplicable, it became a serious question as to what had best be done. The majority were for putting him out of the way offhand, as the others had been served; but when they recalled the rock-keeper's words, and his expressed desire that the child should be disposed of summarily, they hesitated, on the ground that the advice of an enemy may not always be followed with safety. At all events, there could be no great harm in permitting the child to live; he was much too young to notice or remember the events of that night, and if it was true that harm was to come to the Randan tribe through the totem of the young Omiaye, why, without doubt, the longer the said totem was held subject to the body to which it belonged the better.

And now I must again snip the thread of my story while I explain to the reader what a *totem* is. Every North American Indian has one, and his manner of obtaining it is as follows:—While he is still a little child, say of four or five years old, he is led to the depths of the forest, where a tree is selected and a comfortable couch of woven withes, and moss, and leaves constructed in the branches of it. In this bed the child is laid, and there he must remain night and day, without food or drink, until he dreams "the dream of his life," that is, a dream in which there conspicuously appears some beast, or fish, or bird, and whichever it may be, that is the young Indian's totem during the remainder of his life,— the incarnation of his good genius. Say it is a hawk that acts a prominent part in the dreamer's dream of life, for ever after hawks are safe from his arrow; and should he kill one by accident, he would put himself into even deeper mourning than though his father were dead, and in all probability sacrifice a toe or a little finger to it by way of penance. On the other hand, the totem is expected to exercise a potent and salutary influence over the man's life—to warn him of danger and the treachery of enemies. When the man dies, then his totem is free to avenge on its late proprietor's enemies any insult or injury he may have sustained while in the flesh; or if the owner of a totem finds himself growing old and feeble, and unable of his own unaided exertions to consummate a long-cherished plan of revenge, then by supplication and sacrifice he may induce his totem to co-operate with him while he is still alive. Now the sacred rock-keeper's grandson, who was christened Tantivyio, had been put to bed in the Omiaye forest just before the terrible catastrophe already related, and he had dreamt his dream of life and secured his totem.

The Grand Medicine of the Randans was the little boy whom the sacred rock-keeper had cast out of the burning hut. By what arts and stratagems—being an alien—he had attained so high a position would occupy too much space here to enter on. He was crafty, he was cunning, and he was patient. He was humble too, and apparently without any other thought than the welfare of the tribe that had so generously adopted him; but above all he was a hypocrite of the first water, and all the time—ever since, as he lay in the blanket at the rock-minder's hut, he heard him utter his singular prophecy—his heart had been filled with the bitterest hatred against the Randans.

But, and as before stated, to look on him one would never suspect that he had a single care or trouble on his mind, and least of all one that involved a dearth of victuals. Amongst a company of such lean men his obesity was a reproach, as he himself felt and expressed; but that he was not in the least to blame for it everybody was bound to admit, since, so far from availing himself of the privilege of his high order to eat and drink at the expense of whomsoever he pleased, he ate scarcely anything at all. The handful of corn that barely served to keep life in another man from morning till night, lasted Tantivyio a week, and even then he had a few grains left to give to any poor fellow who was famishing. Meat he never indulged in. Stag's flesh he had always avoided, declaring that the least bit of it made him seriously ill; but now all meats were alike to him, and he would not so much as moisten his few grains of parched corn with a little pemican or buffalo-marrow, lest folks should say that it was by such means that he grew fat. What he desired to impress on the people was, that he was a Grand Medicine of such irreproachable character that the gods specially favoured him, and caused food to be conveyed into his stomach while he slept at night by invisible agency; and this seemed not improbable, since every morning when he made his appearance his face invariably wore the expression of a man who has just taken his fill of food of a sort he is extremely fond of. On such occasions, when they offered him things to eat, he would shrug his fat shoulders and piously raise his staggy eyes and say, "I have already breakfasted," though that they knew was impossible, at least in a worldly sense, for the little tent he slept in, and which was removed some distance from the rest (as is the custom of Grand Medicines in order that their pious meditations may not be disturbed), contained not even so much as the usual deer-hide blanket which in these hard times was not unfrequently found nibbled all round by the hungry little children, who, put to bed supperless, could not go to sleep.

So there in the great council-tent sat Tantivyio the Grand Medicine, next to the seat of honour that was occupied by the sage and mighty chief Chypchaney, and the other warriors were reclining here and there on their skin rugs, and in a distant corner crouched Pitchanicker, son of Nuckledown, whose marvellous exploits amongst the Leepfrogs have been already narrated.

For awhile nothing was heard but the soft puffing at pipes—not of tobacco, alas! even that necessary of life in such a season of poverty was not attainable, and the braves were reduced to smoking dried clover—when presently the sage Chypchaney spoke, in so low a whisper, however, that it was with difficulty that even the quick-eared Pitchanicker caught the words—

"Has aught of late been seen of the antlered mystery?"

There was a slight rustling sound in the corner where Pitchanicker crouched, but no other; no one answered the chief's question, though many were the eyes turned in nervous terror towards the tent door.

Then Tantivyio, the fat Grand Medicine, spoke.

"It were well, O chief," said he, "that as little as possible be said concerning the mystery in question, if it exists, which I, who should know as well as any, have doubts of. Since, however, if it does exist, to see it and to speak of it is to die, it were as well that it were not mentioned."

The Grand Medicine spoke in even a lower whisper than the chief had used, but his words were felt by all who heard them, and they cowered still more closely around the fire. It was true. A fortnight since, a warrior, whom business of an urgent nature took abroad late at night, hurried in and roused the camp to tell them of the frightful sight he had witnessed—a spectre elk of proportions so gigantic that his legs were taller than the height of the tallest man, scudding over the pasture land, his enormous mouth open, and his jaws working with the speed of lightning as he, flitting like a ghost, browsed on the parched herbage. The tribe were filled with horror and amazement, and next morning—they had gone to his tent that same night, but he was either too sound asleep to hear them or else disinclined to come out into the cold—the Grand Medicine was applied to for a solution of the mystery, and he merely laughed and said that the man who pretended that he had seen the strange sight must be mad, and that he had better take a little physic to cool his blood. And the man took the physic, and the same night he died. Three nights after, an old squaw, having a sick child to nurse, ventured out after the camp had retired for the night to fetch a jar of water, and she came back squalling and screaming with the selfsame tale the man whose blood needed cooling had told. It is not recorded whether the Grand Medicine physicked her, but she too died some time in the course of the following day. And only the night previous to that on which Chypchaney and his braves sat in council a third person had seen the startling apparition. This was Pitchanicker. He was not abroad by accident when he saw it. He was as shrewd as he was courageous, and when he heard these strange stories of the spectre elk it set him pondering and cementing together all sorts of odd bits of evidence and scraps of suspicion that had long troubled his mind, and the result was that when once more the weary camp was wrapped in slumber he had stolen out of his tent and out on to the desolate prairie. What he saw this is not a fitting place to reveal, but when at grey of morning he stole back to his tent he looked older by a year and more, and full of wonder and amazement. But he made no outcry. Even when Chypchaney asked the question, "Had any one of late seen the antlered mystery?" he still held his peace; but his fiery eyes sought and met those of the Grand Medicine, and the staggy optics of the latter blinked and winked in a highly-embarrassed manner, and at last drooped their fringes to shield them from Pitchanicker's consuming gaze. Later in the evening, when the subject of the phantom elk was forgotten, or at least avoided according to the advice of Grand Medicine, the worthy last mentioned came over to Pitchanicker, and begged his acceptance of a little of his magic snuff, the merest pinch of which would insure such sound sleep as was never before enjoyed. Pitchanicker, concealing his real feelings, accepted the gift with many thanks, but when he reached his tent he prudently tried a pinch of the snuff on his dog, and sure enough it sent the animal to sleep so soundly that it never woke again.

After this Pitchanicker was more than ever convinced that Tantivyio was in some way concerned with the mystery of the spectre elk; still it was a rash thing to bring so serious an accusation against a Grand Medicine man, and he resolved to give the matter further and deliberate consideration. Meanwhile the winter crept on, and frost arrested the running waters, and the river and the lakes were firm to walk on as the earth. This spectacle, the first morning that Pitchanicker saw it, put a new idea into his head.

"My totem is the seal," said he, "and on that account I have never in the hardest seasons been out to trap seals; now, however, I will go, not to kill them, but in hope to get close enough to one to question him as to this rascally Omiaye."

So that nobody might watch his movements he strolled away for a considerable distance until he came to a lonely part of the frozen lake, and then he hacked a hole in the ice with his tomahawk, and sat down by the side of it till such time as a seal came up to breathe. He sat with his hatchet raised, not to make a chop at the first seal's nose he saw thrust up out of the hole, but so that he might administer to it a blow only hard enough to stun it (for which assault it would be easy to apologise when they came to understand each other), and then to secure it until it came to its senses sufficiently to answer any question that might be put to it.

It was horribly cold work squatting down on the ice with an empty stomach and the wind blowing nor'-east, but Pitchanicker was a man of iron resolution, and never budged an inch from sunrise until the shades of evening began to fall. Then was his patience and perseverance rewarded. For the eighty-seventh time he had stirred the water in the hole with the handle of his tomahawk to prevent it setting, when suddenly a slight gurgling sound was heard, and a brown snout rose to the surface.

Pitchanicker was about to strike, but the seal, winking one of its expressive eyes, arrested his upraised arm.

"Forbear, Pitchanicker, son of Nuckledown," said the seal; "do not strike thy totem. All day long have I known thy intention, and but waited at the bottom of the lake, just under this breathing-hole, to test thy patience. Now I have come. What wouldst thou with me?"

This familiar and friendly style of address on the part of his totem at once placed Pitchanicker at his ease.

"My business shall be briefly stated, O seal," replied the young brave. "Thou knowest Tantivyio?"

"Grand Medicine of thy tribe?"

"Right."

"Grandson of the keeper of the pipe-stone rock of the Omiayes?"

"Right again, O my totem."

"Well, what about him?"

"'Tis not concerning him so much, O my totem, as another matter I would gain information from thee. Canst tell me aught of the phantom elk?"

"Not half a moon since these eyes saw it," answered the seal, bobbing his head up a little higher out of the water to indicate the eyes he alluded to. "It came down here to drink. It is thinner than of yore, that phantom elk; it must wait till the spring and the green crops come again, then it will once more grow fat and sleek."

Pitchanicker caught his breath, which the last remark of his totem had well-nigh started out of his body. Still he was too cunning to speak out his thoughts even to his totem.

"Our Grand Medicine was fatter by far a month since than he is now," said he; "one might suppose that he and the phantom elk were related."

PITCHANICKER WATCHING FOR HIS TOTEM.

"One would not be far out if he did think so!"

"How?"

"Canst thou keep a secret that thy totem will disclose to thee?" asked the seal in solemn tones.

"With my life," replied Pitchanicker.

"Then Tantivyio and the phantom elk are one!" whispered the seal, guarding his mouth with his right flipper lest even the wind should catch and carry away the astounding revelation. "Listen, Pitchanicker. If this Tantivyio was of our tribe I would suffer myself to be speared ere I would have revealed his secret; but he is a stranger, an Omiaye, and, fair-speaking though he may appear, a thorn in the foot of every good Randan. He is the last of his race, and it is his accursed mission, sanctioned, alas! by the gods as a punishment for the rash outrage of the Randans against the sacred pipe-stone rock, to work any manner of mischief against our tribe he and his totem can devise. The doings of totems are known to each other, and so I know that Tantivyio, despairing of compassing his spite fully as he could wish against you, prayed to his totem to assist him while he was yet in the flesh, and his totem agreed; with what result is already known to you."

So saying, the seal caught Pitchanicker by the hand, and giving it a friendly squeeze, was about once more to sink to its watery home, when the young Indian, grasping it by one ear, arrested it.

"Tell me, O my totem," said he, "do this villainous Omiaye and the gluttonous elk act in concert, or distinctly?"

"As one," spoke the seal. "At night Tantivyio steals to the forest, and there his totem meets him, and they blend and assume one shape; so that Tantivyio is as guilty of eating up the grass and the corn as the elk his totem."

"That, then, accounts for the rascal's fatness, for his deer-like expression of eye," spoke Pitchanicker; "I see it all now. But one more question, good seal—when does he return to his natural shape?"

"When the earliest bird of the forest begins to chirp," replied the seal, "then the accursed partnership is dissolved, and the elk takes the form of an ash-tree, and Tantivyio skulks back to his hut."

And tired of being held up by the ear while he underwent examination, at this point the seal slipped through Pitchanicker's fingers and plunged down to the bottom of the lake like a stone.

For a time the young Indian was so completely bewildered that he knew not what to do. It was by this time growing late, and the moon had risen.

"It is nine long miles between this and the tents of my tribe," mused he, "and hurry as I may I shall certainly be too late to see the outgoing of this eater-up of a people's bread, but I shall be in time to catch him returning, with a good two hours to spare."

So saying he sat down on a wayside rock, and spent the said two hours in resting his weary legs, and grinding an edge keen as a razor to his tomahawk.

The job completed to his satisfaction, he arose much refreshed, and in less than two

THE ELK DEMON. 79

hours came in sight of the tents of his tribe, of his own tent, and the tent of the villainous Grand Medicine, concerning whom he had heard such astonishing revelations. The chirping of the earliest bird in the forest might shortly be expected; therefore he stole to the tent of Tantivyio, and, peeping in, found it empty. Without hesitation he stepped inside and balanced his sharp and faithful tomahawk in his hand against the return of the enemy of his tribe.

Presently peering through a narrow slit in the canvas, he saw him coming, creeping on all-fours, with a diabolical grin on his fat, full-fed face, and with his eyes more deer-like than ever. The provoking spectacle was too much for Pitchanicker; he could remain in hiding no longer, but uttering his war yell, he bounded out of the tent, flourishing his hatchet.

Fatal imprudence! had he waited but another minute his enemy would have been safely within his grasp, but now he had a chance of escape, and he made the most of it. Soon as Pitchanicker emerged from the tent door he perceived him, and leaping to his feet, turned his face in the direction he had come, and ran. Tantivyio was a swift runner. Before he had grown so monstrously fat there was not his match amongst the Randans; but his increased size was certainly against him, and the pursuit would without doubt have been but of short duration—for Pitchanicker was an excellent runner too—had not the latter but recently returned from a nine miles' journey, to say nothing of his being considerably weakened by his long and hungry watching on the ice; so that, as the matter stood, the match was as equal as possible.

It was a tremendous chase. As Pitchanicker grew warm to his work his pace increased, and as Tantivyio grew warm to *his* work, he took to perspiring so profusely that every hundred yards he ran made him a pound lighter at least, and so increased his chances. Scarcely had the earliest bird in the forest uttered its first twitter when they started, and the ruddy sun of winter was high in the heavens and still Tantivyio was running for his life, as was his deadly enemy, whose fury had not bated one jot; indeed, he had never ceased during the long pursuit to utter his war-cry and flourish his tomahawk. At times he so closely approached him, that could he have depended on his aim he might have flung his weapon and floored Tantivyio with the greatest ease; but in his breathless condition he felt that his aim was not to be depended on, so he still yelled and kept up the chase.

On and still on until noon became afternoon, and still the pursuit continued. It would not have been nearly so protracted only that by a blunder Tantivyio made a false turn to the south instead of the west, and ran several miles before he found an opportunity to alter his course, so closely was he pressed from behind. By this time you would scarce have known him, every ounce of his fat having evaporated in perspiration, leaving him as thin, at least, as his pursuer, and enabling him to give him a taste of his old style of running.

It has been said that Tantivyio made a blunder and turned to the south, when his

PITCHANICKER PURSUES THE ELK MAN.

proper course was due west. But why? Were not all courses the same to him, since his only aim was to outstrip or tire out his relentless enemy? Was that his only aim?
No.

His aim was to reach that northern part of the forest where stood his totem disguised in the shape of an ash-tree until night, when he would assume his demon form and scour the unhappy country, seeking what he might devour. It was not yet night, but Tantivyio was a desperate man, and there was a chance that his totem might stretch a point to serve him.

The ash-tree of the elk totem was of peculiar shape, and might be known from those surrounding it from the circumstance of its first two jutting limbs spreading out like horns. In the distance Tantivyio marked the tree and hailed it with a joyous yell, for by this time he was nearly spent, and his only comfort was that he could not hear the noise of his own blowing because of a louder noise of an exactly similar description constantly audible close to his heels.

But Pitchanicker was ignorant of what Tantivyio was yelling about. " Unless he imagines himself more at home here in the heart and thickness of the forest than I am, and hopes to give me the slip: we shall see," thought Pitchanicker, and mustering his breath, he echoed Tantivyio's yell of triumph.

But the unhappy young Indian was altogether unprepared for the sudden shock in store for him. In a few seconds the ash with the antlered boughs was reached, and with a loud cry to his totem to help him Tantivyio sprang into it; when lo! in an instant Indian and tree vanished, and there appeared in their place the demon elk Pitchanicker had seen on one previous occasion, but now looking a hundred times more ferocious, with an upright ridge of hair extending the full length of its back, and its protruding eyes aglow with consuming wrath. For an instant it glared on Pitchanicker, who had sunk to the earth with horror and exhaustion, and then with an unearthly bellow it bounded away.

What could Pitchanicker do? Even had he been fresh for the chase, and the elk but an ordinary elk, he was armed only with a tomahawk and a scalping-knife, efficient weapons enough when brought against a mere fellow-creature, but next to no good at all towards elk-hunting. " He will escape! The enemy of my tribe has circumvented me, and there is nothing left but for me to return and relate the story of my own defeat." And when the young brave said this he cast himself with his face to the earth and shed bitter tears.

But he had not shed more than eighteen or twenty, when suddenly he raised his head and listened intently. He looked to the right and to the left, and all round about him, but failing to discover what he sought in any direction he laid his face to the earth again, and remained for several seconds without motion.

Had his countenance been visible, however, marvellous was the change that would have appeared on it. But a moment since it was a woe-begone, despairing face, wet with weeping; now it was a bright and eager face, full of hope revived. And why? The totem of Pitchanicker had spoken to him. The strange sound that had disturbed him when he lay down to cry was the sound of the imprisoned waters of the river sighing out at the holes in the ice the seal-fishers had made. Finding this to be the case, Pitchanicker dismissed

THE ELK DEMON.

the matter from his mind, and once more was about to plunge to the depths of that grief from which he had momentarily emerged, when his quick ear detected another sound besides the sighing of the water. It was the sound of a voice with whose tones he was familiar; it was his totem's voice that addressed him. It is marvellous for how long a distance the earth will convey sound! The river was a mile and a quarter away at the very least, and yet the seal applying his mouth to the bank of it, his words were conveyed to Pitchanicker with perfect distinctness. To be sure, seals that are totems may have powers of voice denied to seals of the common breed.

"Rise, O Pitchanicker, son of Nuckledown," thus spoke the totem to the young brave; "the courage thou hast displayed shall not go unrewarded if I can help thee. Cast thine eyes in the direction whence my voice proceeds, and see what thou shalt see."

And Pitchanicker, springing to his feet, did cast his eyes as directed, and what he saw was the frozen river and the demon elk floundering and sliding about on the surface in his endeavours to reach the other side. As the young Randan beheld the curious spectacle his frame seemed to be endowed with new life, and raising his war-cry he rushed once more to the chase. He rushed in such a hurry that he left his tomahawk behind, and, missing it when he had run about a quarter of a mile, was returning for it, but a voice, blending with the wind, and which was unmistakably that of the totem seal, cried, "On, on, don't turn back;" so he kept on, trusting his totem implicitly.

Nor was his faith unrewarded. Reaching the brink of the frozen river with a bound and a yell he leaped upon it, and, being an excellent slider, in less than a minute was far from the shore, with his face full of stern resolution turned towards the spot where the demon elk was still floundering and slipping. So intently did he fix his gaze on the object of his hatred, that he well-nigh slid into a hole in the ice that lay directly in his path. Indeed, so closely did he approach it that he thrust out his hands to save himself, when, behold! at the same instant there shot up out of the hole a spear-shaft, and his hands grasped it, and next instant, with hearty thanks to his kind totem, he was scudding along again with such a weapon in his hands as the mightiest elk-hunter in the land might have envied.

And if ever a man needed such a weapon, it was Pitchanicker at that time. It was no ordinary animal he had to contend against, but a creature of gigantic proportions and strength, and with a magic life that no spear of a common order could damage. Cheered by his new possession, Pitchanicker renewed his exertions, as did the demon elk, and with so much success that ere the young Indian could reach it, it had gained the shore. Pitch-

THE ELK DEMON AT BAY.

THE ELK DEMON. 87

anicker was very vexed when he saw this. "He will have the advantage now that he has got on land again, and will doubtless lead me as pretty a dance as I have been engaged in all day."

But he was mistaken: the demon elk had not the remotest intention of running away. Why should he from such an insignificant foe as that who pursued him? It might have been a little awkward to charge him and trample him to bits on the slippery ice, but now it was quite another matter. And as Pitchanicker leaped to the shore, the demon elk, turning short about with glaring eyes, made a dead charge against the young Randan.

And now indeed did the magic spear with which Pitchanicker's totem had supplied him stand his good friend. Coolly as though he was exercising in the playground of his tribe, the Randan grasped the spear to receive the thundering charge, and never heeding it, the elk came on. But the result was somewhat different from what the latter reckoned on. With full confidence in his magic hide, the elk scorned the huntsman's spear as though it had been but a reed, and thought only of the pleasure of goring this insolent Randan, and mashing and smashing him. But the spear as well as the hide was magic, and when they met, the former pierced the latter at the breast part, so that the spear-head was hidden to the first shaft-feathers, and at the same moment the air was rent by a cry of a man, and not of an elk, and Pitchanicker grinned as he recognised the voice of Tantivyio, who doubtless had all unexpectedly been progged in his seclusion.

But the demon elk was not yet subdued. Without doubt he was very much astonished, which at least was lucky for Pitchanicker, since the brute, starting back in its amazement, released the Randan's spear, the shaft of which he still grasped firmly in his hands. It was clear from the expression of the elk's eye that he was aware that he was fighting against magic, whether more potent than his own remained to be seen. Once more he charged, leaping high in the air, with the intention of coming down all-fours and with his sharp hoofs gathered to a bunch on Pitchanicker's devoted head. But that wily young Indian knew better. Throwing up his spear at the exactly proper moment, he caught the malicious beast a dig in the haunch that caused him to fling his legs out broad astraddle and to leap forward with such heartiness that he was carried sheer over Pitchanicker's head, and several feet beyond. And finding himself so completely baffled, with a roar of rage and pain he scrambled to his legs again and sought safety in flight.

Now was the victory half won. Totem and demon though he was, the elk had acknowledged the superiority of the Randan brave, and fled before him. This thought inspired the young man with threefold ardour and courage, and with a rejoicing yell he set off in pursuit with the speed of the wind. On, on, till the darkness of night fell, on till the moon rose, still the demon elk showed no signs of flagging, neither did Pitchanicker, for the spear his totem had given him was of itself a charm against fatigue. On over plain and hill, and through forest and brake, never ceasing. Sometimes the path the elk took was so intricate that for a time his pursuer lost sight of him, but he invariably left his track behind him; he was wounded fore and aft, and every movement of his body caused the blood to trickle.

At last, and all unexpected, there was an end to the chase. As previously explained, it was only from dark till earliest dawn that the wicked Grand Medicine was allowed to incorporate with the elk his totem, and though the rule had been infringed to a certain extent on the previous evening, it was an infringement that might not be repeated. Though he must have lost blood enough to have filled the arteries of twenty ordinary elks, this one seemed fresh as ever, and with life in him yet for a twenty miles run. But it was not to be. All of a sudden, and just as dawn began to peep through the dun clouds, there was a rustling in the boughs overhead, and the demon elk pricked up his ears nervously. Following instantly on the rustling the piping of the earliest bird in the forest was heard, and so unexpectedly that Pitchanicker nearly stumbled over him, the elk stood still as a stone, while his antlers assumed a green tinge like the green of a tree, plainly indicating that the animal was about to take its customary disguise for the day. An instant's delay and all the young hunter's pain and trouble would go for nothing. There was no instant's delay. Nerving his arms for the deadly thrust, the Randan charged with all his force at the elk's heart, and blending with its death-groan was heard the agonised cry of a mortally-wounded man, and there lay Tantivyio and his totem food for crows.

*   *   *   *   *   *   *

Within three days the magic spear hung in the most conspicuous part of the great wigwam of the Randans, and Pitchanicker, attired in the robes of Grand Medicine, sat at the right hand of the sage chief Chypchaney, and from that time never again did the crops of the Randans fail or their children cry for bread.

BLACK STONE SPITE.

really possessing no small amount of either, passing as handy-man and gossip merely, humble and harmless, respected by all and trusted by all—even by those who had given Wangeleye very grave secrets to keep.

A very pretty history might be written concerning this crafty comb-maker, and the many wicked and daring things he did all the while that he was hoodwinking the people; but this is no place for the account. He kept his mask on without the least slip to the last, and now, as before stated, that he lay on his mat dying of an ague, his relatives and friends, including the king's physician, were gathered about him sympathising and condoling. His end was rapidly approaching, as might be easily judged from the fact that they had already dressed his hair, and painted his face, and rubbed him with scented oil, so that he might go to the grave as handsome as possible. And now they stood round his mat waiting in breathless silence for him to declare his future shape.

It is a custom amongst these people, or, more correctly speaking, a religious necessity, to declare what their future shape shall be before they die, in order that their relatives may recognise and pay due respect to it ever afterwards. It is a savage sort of confessional indeed—a "throwing out," as they call it. If he never in his life told the truth before, it is expected and demanded of a man when on his death-bed. And it is never expected in vain, since the man has nothing to dread of his earthly enemies, and all to dread of the gods who will presently have to judge him. At the last solemn "throwing out," and never before, may a man's friends know him. It is not for him to choose his future shape: the quality of the life he has led settles that question for him, and the various natures and forms of things are emblematic of the crimes man in his wickedness may commit. As, for instance, if a man has been guilty of no great crime, he will elect to take for the future some pleasant shape, such as a tall palm or growing corn, or a bird, a star, or any one of a hundred other shapes; but if he has been specially guilty now it will come out. If he has been a common murderer, the white shark is the only shape for him; if he has stolen goods of the king, he may choose to be nothing else than a monkey; if he has committed the most monstrous crime of all—that of secretly murdering any member of the royal family or a priest of the temple—then he is for ever doomed to be a snake, a pig, or a rotten yam; and so on as regards all manner of degrees of iniquity.

"Tell us, O Wangeleye, what thy future shape shall be," said his uncle, taking his hand affectionately. "Thou hast, as all men know, observed a life that is without reproach. Be a moon, my nephew, and then we can look up at night, and say, 'There shines our kinsman,' and hold up our little children that they may admire and take example."

But the dying comb-cutter impatiently snatched away his hand, and groaned as he turned his face to the wall.

"Be a flower, my father!" cried his youngest daughter—"a flower of sweet smell, that the wind may be thy messenger, and cry as it blows in far-off places, 'I carry the breath of Wangeleye, the sweet breath of the king's comb-cutter.'"

But the old man only groaned the louder, and dismally shook his head.

"Be a tortoise, master!" exclaimed his old apprentice Smorltuth, who, knowing the old man's ways, thought that his disinclination to name his future shape arose out of his reluctance to leave his present one with all its luxurious surroundings. "Be a tortoise, and join the shoals of precious shell-yielders that live in the sea, and when I die," continued the faithful fellow, "I will be a sharp saw, and I will come to thee, and we will do such a trade together as never two comb-cutters did before."

But the dying man could be none of these shapes. He was seized with a fit of trembling that he knew presaged his end; so not daring to face his family, he beckoned his apprentice to come the side to which his face was turned.

"My faithful Smorltuth!" said he, in a voice quivering with emotion, "I may be neither a flower, nor a moon, nor a tortoise. Would that I might, were it only a moon in its last quarter or the common flower of the sweet potato. No, Smorltuth, the terrible truth must be thrown out, the loathsome shape must be declared: I will be a snake!"

Had his words been, "I am stuffed with gunpowder, and this moment I swallowed a match," the consternation amongst his relatives could not have been more sudden or complete. The cry they uttered was as one cry, and the rush that was made for the door (which was of quilted skins) tore it down, and it was trampled on the threshold. Even the faithful Smorltuth drew back from his old master, and would doubtless have fled with the others had not horror and amazement bereft him of the use of his limbs. Presently, however, he sufficiently recovered to exclaim—

"No, no, my master, not that horrible shape—not the shape of the worst of murderers! While there is yet time unsay the terrible words. Be a shark, a monkey even, but not a snake!"

But Smorltuth was in error when he spoke of there being yet time. It was time past now with the court comb-cutter: he was dead.

The news spread like wildfire. People who had all along placed implicit confidence in Wangeleye, and never for a moment doubted that he was as worthy a fellow as ever lived, now suddenly recollected that he had always worn a haggard and anxious look, as though something of terrible weight was burdening his conscience, while others had a distinct remembrance of his agitation when the old queen died, and again when the Princess Stiklikrish was found poisoned in her bed. Three years previously the chief priest of the temple had broken a blood-vessel which caused his death, and now it was whispered that he had not broken it at all, but that it was Wangeleye's work, and that he therefore was responsible for the calamity. There was only one individual who stood out stoutly for the old comb-maker's innocence, declaring that he was out of his mind when he accused himself, and that no notice should be taken of his demand to be regarded in future as a snake. This was Wangeleye's son-in-law; but so far from mending matters, the young man's undisguised expression of his opinion rather aggravated them, since his rebellious behaviour towards all recognised law and authority, his ridicule of many most serious and solemn rites and ceremonies of the nation, had already made him a marked man, and though he was one of the best soldiers in the king's army, there is little doubt that his life would have been long ago forfeited had it not been for his relationship with the king's favourite.

When the news of the court comb-maker's confession came to the king's ears his anger knew no bounds—not that Wangeleye should be so monstrously wicked, but that he should be such a fool, the truth being that, availing himself of his great confidence in his gossip, he had commissioned him in three or four matters of a very delicate nature—the putting out of the way of the Princess Stiklikrish amongst the number—and he was mortally afraid that popular curiosity might be roused, and certain facts come out calculated to breed unpleasantness between himself and his subjects. More than all he was afraid of Djujube, the son-in-law of Wangeleye already mentioned, since he knew not how deeply he might be acquainted with the old comb-maker's private affairs. The result was that his majesty passed a sleepless night, and in the morning he called a cabinet council, and informed it of his determination, by way of example, and to prevent a recurrence of such treacherous atrocity, to banish Wangeleye and his kith and kin, every man, woman, and child of them, to Black Stone Island.

"And take care that they are lodged at *this end* of it," said his majesty, "so that the next time the stone-bearer travels that way he may make a speedy journey."

BLACK STONE SPITE.

The council were amazed at the severity of the royal sentence, and, after whispering, asked of the king whether the valiant warrior Djujube was to be reckoned among the banished.

"Lodge him and his family in the first hut," replied the king significantly. And so the council dispersed, not daring to dispute his majesty's commands.

Does the reader know what banishment to Black Stone Island implied? He shall be informed.

In those good old times the inhabitants of Figi and the surrounding islands had great faith in human blood as a means of cementing their friendship with the gods. When the king's palace was built the doorposts rested in a fresh pool of the vital fluid; when the great temple was erected the twelve tremendous pillars of it were each grounded on the body of a human victim. The launching of a royal canoe, the birth or death of a royal child, a start for the battle-field or a return from the same, a dearth of rain or a superabundance of it, and countless other occurrences, each demanded its human sacrifice, so that in humdrum, peaceable times, when few prisoners of war were taken, the priests were at their wits' ends for victims. It was to meet this difficulty that Black Stone Island was colonised. It was a small tract of land not more than a mile across, and fruitful and picturesque as any in Polynesia; but its inhabitants were the most miserable that can be imagined, and no wonder, since they were all marked for death. There are no prisons in this part of the world, nor the least occasion for *habeas corpus* law. If a man committed a crime deserving of death he was clubbed out of hand or banished to the island in question, there to remain, like an ox at grass, till required for slaughter. Why it was called Black Stone Island was because whenever a victim or victims were required the messengers came bearing a queerly-shaped stone, black in colour, and the like of which was not to be found in all the world. Indeed, this one was not found in the world, but—so the priests averred—was dropped from the clouds by the gods to serve this special purpose.

Djujube was married and had one child, a dear little boy, whom he loved more than all the world besides, excepting his wife. When he heard the king's commands he laughed scornfully, and snapped his fingers at the contents of the document, as the messenger read it out to him; but when, an instant afterwards, it occurred to him that his fate involved that of the two innocent and helpless beings dependent on him, his brow grew cloudy, and something like a tear obscured his vision. It was on his tongue's tip, for their sakes, to entreat the king's mercy; only for a moment, however, did this idea possess him; the next he dashed the tear from his eye, and with his teeth set determinedly and a more scornful laugh than before, he bade the messenger lead the way to the great sailing-canoe already waiting to convey him and his wife and all her relations to the fatal island.

"Which is my hut?" Djujube demanded of the officers as he landed.

"The first hut; the king has regard for you, and doubtless will soon send a messenger to inquire after your health," the officer replied, laughing at his brutal joke.

"I trust when that happens I may be able to report my muscles as strong and healthy as my will," replied Djujube grimly. Thinking that this, too, was a joke, the officer began to laugh again, but catching the sinister expression of the doomed man's eyes he broke off suddenly, and turned his laugh to a whistle.

"Did you hear what Djujube said?" remarked this officer to another, as, having deposited their cargo, the crew was returning to the sailing-canoe.

"What of it?"

"More than seems, you may depend. We shall hear of him again, if I am not mistaken."

"I fully expect to," laughed the other, "and that shortly. The feast of taro (a sort of harvest-home, on getting in the taro crop) takes place next week, and then we shall meet him and taste him too, if we are lucky."

Djujube heard nothing of this conversation, but he knew as well as any man concerning the times of feasts and festivals, and already in his own mind he had reckoned when the king's vengeance against him would be fully gratified. "There are always three victims at the taro feast," thought he, "and myself, and my wife, and my darling little Towsclair are the three already marked, I have no doubt. We shall see."

But he revealed nothing of his dismal forebodings to his wife. When she asked him why they were placed in the first hut in the village, he replied that it was because it was the most comfortable and airy, being nearest the sea. Of course she knew the horrid fate to which they were destined, but the island, at that time, happened to be very well stocked with people, and therefore no immediate danger, so she thought, need be apprehended.

But Djujube knew better, and took his measures accordingly. Soon as they were settled in the hut he got two spades and two digging-sticks, and bade his wife help him dig a deep pit all across one side of the floor, and when she asked him the purpose of the pit, he informed her that it was to store yams in for the winter. This answer reassured her in her previous conjectures that death might be a long distance from them as yet, and so she set to work with a will, and, though the ground was very hard, within three days they had made a hole nine feet deep, and six wide, and eight broad. The earth they took out of the hole they carried down to the seashore at night-time, and by the morning the tide had carried it all away, so that when Djujube placed splints of wood across and across

DJUJUBE SETS OUT TO FISH FOR HIS EXPECTED FRIENDS.

the mouth of the hole, and spread over this rushes, as the remainder of the floor was spread, there was nothing without or within the hut to show that there was any pit at all.

The day before the feast of taro, Djujube said to his wife, "Kill a little pig and have it ready baked, while I will go fishing, so that you may make some nice vy-hoo (fish soup), and a dish, after your best manner, of loolo-feki (dried cat-fish), stewed in cocoa-milk; for to-morrow I expect friends."

So, although she wondered much who the friends could possibly be, she asked no questions, but saluted him after the custom of the country, and wished him good luck, and then set about doing as her husband bade.

Before sunrise next morning Djujube was stirring. "You lie still," said he to his wife, as he came from the inner to the outer chamber; "I am going to spread the feast for my friends, whom I expect shortly."

But when by-and-by she got up and came into the chamber where they took their food, she discovered that her husband had set out the feast just over the covered pit, and, moreover, that, trailing along the floor and carelessly hitched to two hooks driven in the wall, were two ropes of twisted bark. She was about to ask what it meant, but Djujube, by an authoritative glance, instantly checked her; so she set about her household duties as though nothing was the matter.

Presently Djujube, looking out at his door that faced the sea, cried, "My friends are coming." On which his wife looked out also, and as she did so she clapped both her hands over her mouth to save herself from shrieking aloud, and trembled down on to her knees, for within a mile of the island she saw two canoes with two men in each, and from their shape and colour she at once knew them to be the canoes of the Black Stone priests; and she needed no telling what their mission was.

"And are these thy friends, O my husband?" cried she, clinging to him. "Are we so old, and grown so tired of each other, and of the sight and company of our darling Towsclair, that we should welcome the messengers of death as friends?"

"Nay, not the messengers of death, the messengers of life and liberty," replied Djujube, embracing her passionately, and affectionately rubbing noses, first with her and then with little Towsclair, who at that instant came toddling in; "compose thyself, and put on a cheerful look, or my guests will be suspicious and avoid my invitation."

So, fully trusting him, she composed herself, and taking her little boy with her carried a jar to the spring to fetch water, that the guests might rinse their mouths and wash their hands. By the time she got back she saw that the two canoes were hauled up on to the beach, and as she entered the hut the four Black Stone officers were there, the chief one carrying in his hand the terrible stone, suspended at the end of a sacred crimson feather.

"Nay, it were idle to eat at present, when so sumptuous a feast will be spread for us in the afternoon," she heard the chief officer say; "you had best follow us at once."

But the other three regarded the spread wistfully, as well they might, for never was a little feast laid out more tastefully. "A mouthful will do us no harm," said one of the fellows; "I never could resist loolo-feki," and as he spoke he dipped his finger into the fragrant hash, and sucked it, and smacked his lips with a relish. "It is the very finest I ever tasted in my life," said he.

This settled the question. The chief officer, too, was passionately fond of loolo-feki, and after a little further wavering he consented to sit down; and with a great show of reverence and humility Djujube waited on them, and placed them at the four corners of the lid that covered the pit. Before sitting down, and to guard against interruption, the chief officer hung the sacred emblem of his office in the doorway.

And so they ate and drank till they were quite merry, their doomed host standing by like a servant, and pouring out palm-wine for them. Presently said the chief officer—

"Drink a cup with us, Djujube; 'twill be thy last, poor fellow. Drink our toast, 'The gods pull and we pull.'"

"With all my heart, my masters," replied Djujube. And as he took the proffered cup he cast a significant glance at his wife, who sidled to the wall; and when the cups were raised, and they were engaged in drinking, Djujube, too, darted to the wall where the ropes were, and snatching at one while his wife snatched at the other, "The gods pull and *I* pull," cried he, and in an instant the false floor parted in the centre, and, with the remains of the feast, and the wine-jar, and the calabashes, down went the four Black Stone priests into the pit. The remainder of Djujube's work was comparatively easy. Seizing his club, as one head after another struggled up in the deep hole, he dealt it one single knock and it struggled no more; after which Djujube replaced the cover of the pit and strewed the rushes over it, and except for a faint odour of wine and baked meat, nothing remained to tell of feast or feasters.

Not a moment was to be lost. In designing and so far carrying out his terrible scheme the young warrior had but one object, and that was to secure the priests' canoes and escape in them to some distant island where their enemies dare not follow them. In a few words he divulged this plan to his wife.

"Get together," said he, "enough of corn and water to keep us on a voyage of a day's duration, and tie up your hair (she had hair very long and luxuriant), so that it may pass as the hair of a man." And while she was making these preparations, Djujube went down to the beach and dragged the bark canoes which were lashed together down to the water. Then he came back and listened at the pit-hole, but all was quiet as though it had been a grave. Then came the most daring part of the business. As already stated, he was a young man of shrewd intellect and advanced opinions, and was not afraid to stigmatise many of the superstitious rites and ceremonies of his fellow-countrymen as rank nonsense. For instance, he did not in the least believe in the sacred origin of the Black Stone. "It answers the purpose of the priests to declare that it came from the gods," Djujube argued with himself; "and I have not the least doubt that if it were lost, it would be some considerable time before they were able to procure a like satisfactory warrant." And as he thought this another idea came into his head. "While I am escaping from the certain death that awaits me, I may as well do a good turn for the poor wretches who are only waiting the Black Stone summons to go to slaughter like a pig to the shambles; I will take the sacred stone away with me." It was a monstrously bold thing to do, but Djujube did it. He folded the stone and the sacred red feather together respectfully, and placed them within the folds of his girdle.

By which time his wife had completed her little arrangements and had fastened up her hair to manly perfection, and then they went down to where the canoes were and got aboard. Meanwhile the trembling inhabitants of the island had remained within with closed doors, peeping through chinks and crevices in the walls to watch for the departure of the Black Stone messengers with their victims. Great was their astonishment, first, at the delay which occurred, and then to see Djujube and a strange man and the child boarding the canoes alone. One or two of the boldest stole out and came down to the beach, when, to their further amazement, they discovered that the supposed strange man was Djujube's wife in disguise.

"And where are the officers?" demanded the wondering few.

"Hush!" said Djujube; "they are still within our hut."

Hearing which the few curious ones started in terror and ran back to their huts for their lives, leaving the coast clear.

Without a moment's hesitation Djujube pushed off, and, with the assistance of his wife, who was a young and muscular woman, very soon put a broad mile of water between the hateful island and their canoes, while the innocent Towsclair sat in the stern of the canoe his mamma was propelling, and by his childish glee and prattle spurred its parents to even more vigorous exertions.

So they rowed might and main till the shades of evening fell, and both were well-nigh faint with weariness, and, as well as Djujube could judge, at least thirty miles must

The Escape from Black Stone Island.

DEUTHE TRIES HIS HAND AS A HUNTSMAN ON THE WONDERFUL ISLAND.

have been gained. But the night closed in and the moon rose ere land appeared, and so weary were they when they stepped ashore, and so glad to lie down on a grassy bank to rest their overstrained limbs, as to be quite forgetful of the necessity of securing the canoes; and when after many hours' heavy sleep they awoke, to their dismay they discovered that with the tide of early morning they had drifted away and were nowhere to be seen.

This was alarming, for on every side of the little island on which they were the sea extended apparently without limit, so that in this respect they were as much prisoners as though still on the fatal Black Stone land. Otherwise their condition was not so deplorable. Their first act was to explore the little island through and through, and, to their great satisfaction, they discovered that, besides themselves, it contained no other human inhabitant, nor, indeed, any trace that such had ever existed there. On the other hand, there was food sufficient for a thousand people, had as many come there. Thousands and tens of thousands of cocoa palms reared their fruitful heads in the wildest luxuriance, while the nuts of last and many a preceding year rotted heaped up on the ground. The squirrels swarmed in the trees, and kangaroos leaped about plentiful as mosquitoes in a mango swamp; the fluttering the birds made was so loud that it was not easy to make the human voice heard, and ever and anon the majestic cassowary broke from cover and startled the air with its shrill cries as it bounded away.

Neither Djujube nor his wife and child had broken their fast since the previous morning. As already related, they had brought away with them provision enough; but such had been their anxiety to make the most of their time, that they had given no thought to eating or drinking, and all the rice, and the cold pig, and the yam they had stowed in the canoes was lost with these vessels. It was fortunate that Djujube had brought ashore his axe and spear, otherwise (for the game on the island was very wild) they might have gone still longer hungry. As it was, however, the larder was easily supplied. Accompanied by his wife and child, the young warrior set out to hunt, and in less than an hour a fine fat young kangaroo and a few smaller quadrupeds of delicate flavour were brought down, with which the party returned in triumph to the spot where they at first landed, and kindled a fire by rubbing sticks together, and in a little while a magnificent roast smoked before them.

And now happened a circumstance that perplexed both the young man and his wife not a little. Djujube was a fair eater, but his wife had but a poor appetite, and an ordinary-sized chicken, with taro pudding and a yam or so, sufficed for her dinner at best of times. As for Towselair, the little a child of his tender years consumes is scarcely worth mention. But now the trio seemed gifted with the appetite of wolves, nay, of ostriches and worse. The kangaroo was not full-sized, certainly, but it was plump and fat, and as much as Djujube's wife could carry, and then there were two animals of the rabbit tribe, and three rats, of which little Towselair was very fond. At any other time the rabbits alone would have served as a tolerable makeshift meal; but now, soon as they were warm through, Djujube seized one and his wife the other, and in a dozen mouthfuls they had vanished. By this time the larger animal was well done enough for eating, and with his hatchet Djujube chopped off one of its hind-quarters, and giving it to his wife, laughingly bade her eat it up if she could, while he gave all his attention to the other hind-quarter. But lo! the meat vanished just as the rabbits had done, and without a word Djujube divided the remainder of the carcass and shared it with his wife, and nothing was heard but mumbling and munching for the space of ten minutes or thereabout, when simultaneously man and wife swallowed their last mouthful, and simultaneously made a hungry grab at a little bit of crackling that had dropped off in the carving.

"Wonderful!" exclaimed Djujube, after they had regarded each other in speechless amazement for several seconds. "I feel as though I had not eaten a bit!"

"And I as though I could eat you almost," replied his wife, smacking her lips hungrily. And as she spoke little Towselair began to cry, and when they inquired the reason, they found that it was because he had devoured his three rats and wanted some more.

"It must be our long sea voyage and going without food all yesterday," said Djujube. "Ha, ha! if we go on at this rate there will be no fear of our enemies recognising us, we shall grow so fat."

So bidding his wife wait a little while the young man started off once more with his spear, and in half-an-hour returned with four more rabbits, three hares, and thirteen birds, great and small, and some of them with plumage so magnificent that it seemed a sin to cast them on the fire; but such was the unaccountable hunger of the family, that the time it would have taken to pluck the birds and to skin the hares and rabbits was grudged, and they were cast down to cook just as they were brought in, and even before they were done they were seized with avidity and torn limb from limb and swallowed, the birds, and the hares, and the rabbits, and after all they sat regarding each other even more famished-looking than before.

"Where was the use in bringing such stupid little things as birds and rabbits?" his wife grumbled; "it is only mockery to a hungry belly. Ah! how hungry I am! I could eat the head of a hippopotamus."

Djujube was hungry too, but he was full of amazement, and that for a time checked the gnawing pains in his stomach. "There's witchery in this," thought he; "this is a witch island, and the creatures that inhabit it are not real, but merely shadows. I wish the canoes had not drifted away."

"It will be growing dark soon, and then you will not be able to see to chase anything," his wife hinted.

"I shall hunt no more to-day," replied Djujube; "I am too tired," and then he lay down, pretending to sleep, but in reality to think over what sort of a witch it was that was haunting the island. Suddenly the origin of the magic occurred to him. All day yesterday, all night, all through the day, he had carried it about with him, and never once given it a thought—the Black Stone in his girdle. There could be no doubt of it. That was the witch. He had thought too lightly of it, he had scoffed at and despised it, and, after all, it was sacred and powerful. He had received the death token, and he must die, him and his wife and son. It was clear that the gods were determined to vindicate their right, as well as their power, by compelling him to starve to death in the midst of plenty. But though he lay trembling and sweating in fear, he still pretended to sleep and take no notice of his wife, when, in the middle of the night, she stole away softly, and shortly returned with half-a-dozen cocoa-nuts, which she cracked and devoured greedily, and without offering him so much as a bit of one, although she knew him to be as hungry as she was.

This was a fresh source of grief to Djujube, since it showed that the curse was extending. His wife had always been most kind and submissive, and now she was greedy and full of bitterness against him. At another time she would have felt the weight of his spear-handle for such an act, but now he only shed tears of sorrow, and did not even rebuke her. All the while the fatal Black Stone rested where he had placed it. He could feel it through the folds of his hip-cloth, pressing against his side as he lay, but for his life's sake he dare not remove it or even lay a finger on it.

Towards morning he dozed to sleep, but was immediately awoke by little Towselair crying for food. So, sadly enough, he got up, and once more took his spear and went off, and speedily returned laden with various sorts of small animals, and bade his wife cook them. But she had not the patience. "Why waste time when we are so hungry?" said she; "the warm blood is in them; they will do well enough," and at once she proceeded to tear them up and devour them like a wild beast, little Towsclair performing his part tooth and nail. She was as greedy now as she had been in the night.

"And am not I to have some breakfast?" asked Djujube, seeing that she drew all the food he had brought towards her.

"Breakfast! do you mean this for breakfast?" she demanded derisively. "I thought it was merely something for our amusement while you went and procured us food more substantial."

So, with a heavy heart, he started off again, and after an absence of nearly two hours returned with two full-grown kangaroos, one over his shoulder and the other dragging at his heels. Then she embraced him and called him by all manner of endearing names, but Djujube was hungrier after meat than caresses, and rudely pushing her away, bade her cook his dinner.

So a great fire was made and the animals roasted, both of them, and they were so large and full of flesh, that, although they were eating their hardest the whole time, it was growing sundown ere either showed symptoms of giving in. At last the woman moved her mouth slower and slower, and presently her hands fell to her sides and she burst into tears.

"How now, wife?" exclaimed Djujube sarcastically; "you surely cannot have eaten enough?"

"No, my husband," she sobbed, "it is not that. It is that such a nice lot of meat is here and my jaws are so weary, that, though I starve before your eyes, I cannot eat another morsel until I have rested."

Djujube, being the stronger, was able to maintain the attack some time longer, but in a short time he, too, was compelled to desist, with every tooth in his head aching from fatigue, but with his appetite as keen as when he first sat down. It was dreaming of eating, and nothing else.

And that day was the first of many, many similar ones. By this time Djujube had rid himself of the fatal Black Stone, and had hidden it along with the sacred red feather under a great stone close down by the beach. To his wife he had never mentioned so much as a word concerning it. He was afraid to do so, since, for all that she was wily old Wangel-eye's daughter, she was full to the eyes of the superstitions of the country, and as likely as not would have fallen down dead of fright had she known of his awful possession. She knew that they were bewitched, she said, and by her cross and snappish behaviour it was evident to Djujube that she regarded the evil as due to him, which made the misfortune all the harder to bear, poor fellow, since, after all, his sole and only object in stealing the stone was that the lives of the wretched inhabitants of the island might be saved, or at least prolonged. But he kept his mouth shut and deigned no sort of explanation. Indeed, he found enough to do, and more than enough, in providing for his increasingly gluttonous appetite, and that of his wife and child. Hour after hour did Djujube spend in the forest hunting and trapping game, with which he would by-and-by come home laden, and this would be hastily cooked—since you may be sure that his wife, who by this time was the image of famine itself, had a fire ready kindled on such occasions—and as hastily devoured, and after a little rest Djujube would be up and off again, to return laden as before; sometimes repeating the tedious process as many as three times between sunrise and dusk of evening.

But, as may be easily imagined, such ceaseless and tremendous drains on the resources of the forest were not to be made with impunity. Of this alarming and melancholy fact the young warrior became each day more and more convinced. Where at first it took him but a short hour to fill with game the great bag of woven grass that his wife had made for the purpose, he now thought himself lucky if it was half filled in the time. At the expiration of two months the very last rabbit was snared, the cunningest monkey—a very old and tough one—was tumbled from his perch in the lofty boughs by a cast of Djujube's sling. A week after that the last rat found an early tomb in the insatiable maw of little Towsclair. As for the birds, they at first were more plentiful that anything, and might have held out a week or so longer, but very naturally they took fright at Djujube's constant onslaught, and made their escape to more secure quarters. There was one species of bird produced on the island that could not fly, and which, on account of its immense bulk, was regarded as a glorious catch by the young Figian, when by luck one fell before his spear. This bird was the cassowary; but at last this bird was swept away—all except one, the giant of his tribe, and fuller of cunning even than the last monkey previously mentioned. Whole days had Djujube employed in endeavouring to circumvent this curiously wide-awake creature, but although it was not in the least shy, and would at times allow the hunter to approach fairly to within spear cast of it, somehow or other he could never hit it, and being so unfortunate as to possess but one spear, by the time he had recovered his weapon the great bird was far out of reach.

At last, excepting this cassowary, there was nothing left alive in the forest but reptiles, and snails, and spiders, and butterflies. The latter flew about in clouds, but what were they, raw or cooked, before such voracious creatures as the Djujubes? So they fell back on the reptiles—the snakes, and worms, and lizards, that made their holes under the roots of the trees; and shocking indeed was the spectacle, and enough to have melted the heart of their worst enemy had he seen them cowering over their spluttering, smoky fire in the evening, devouring, with the greed of ravenous beasts, the loathsome collection of the day.

But such a deplorable condition of affairs could not last. A hundred times a day did Djujube wish that he had let matters take their course in the first instance, then his misery would have been long ago over. It was terrible to see his wife and child dwindling before his eyes, yet what could he do? By night as well as by day he was now abroad, searching for wherewithal to keep life and soul together, and very often returning with no more than sufficed for a meal that might be swallowed in a minute.

At last Djujube's wife fell sick. She was pining of hunger, in fact. Vegetable diet was of not the slightest use to her, and so Djujube found it in his own case, or else there was still abundance of fruit and nuts growing in the forest. She wanted meat, she said, and that was all she did say; and she lay crying for it in a manner that drove her husband beside himself to hear. Nothing in the shape of meat was procurable. That cassowary was still abroad growing fatter and more tempting-looking every day, but the hunter had engaged in so many fruitless attempts to catch it that finally he gave it up as a hopeless task. Little Towselair got on best of the three, since with his tiny hands he could get at the ants' nests in the crevices of the trees, and very frequently made a tolerable breakfast when his parents went hungry.

But the woman would not touch ants even when they were brought to her. She insisted on having meat, and so implored her husband to get her a little—ever so little—so that her mouth might know the flavour of it once more before she died. Djujube shrugged his shoulders, knowing how hopeless it was, but he promised that he would do his best, and beckoning Towselair, who had made himself a spear out of a stick, hardening the point of it in the fire, they set out. But hour after hour passed, and though they poked in all the likely-looking holes in the ground, not so much as a mouse could they discover.

"It is of no use, my son!" exclaimed Djujube, "there is nothing to be found, and

your mother must die without again tasting meat; she will die alone too, for I can never face her again without taking her what her heart is so set on!"

At this the affectionate little fellow began to cry, and to beg his father to take him back to his mother.

"Never without meat in some shape," replied Djujube firmly.

THE LAST OF HIS RACE.

"Oh, meat, meat! where is there meat?" cried the little boy, wringing his hands in agony; but at the same instant he uttered a loud cry of joy, and sprang to the other side of the road, and instantly returning, placed in his father's hands a lizard of large size. It was but a mouthful of meat after all, but never, even when Djujube had bagged a cassowary, did he exhibit so much delight.

Hurrying home, he found his wife just as he had left her, with this astonishing exception, that, coiled by the pillow of grass he had made and placed under her head, was a black snake of considerable size. There was ten times more meat in it than in the lizard, and Djujube was amazed. "She must indeed be nigh to death that she doesn't seize on and devour that beautiful snake," thought he; and with that he approached, and raised his spear to break the snake's head, but with a loud cry she sprang to her feet, and placed herself between her husband and the reptile.

"Nay, do not slay it," said she imploringly. "True, it is the cause of all our misery, my Djujube, but spare it for my sake!"

"How? What? Who?" exclaimed Djujube, more and more bewildered.

"My father!"

Djujube pushed her aside with a gesture of impatience, thinking to be sure that she must be mad. He was awfully hungry himself, and afraid that while his wife was taking on at this insane rate the snake might take opportunity to glide away and escape. But as he raised his spear again the black snake uncoiled itself and reared its head, and then Djujube dropped the weapon and started back in terror. It was indeed his wife's father. It wore a serpent's head and a serpent's face; still there was something about it that stamped it undoubtedly as belonging to Wangeleye, the comb-cutter. Had there been any question in the matter it was speedily answered, for in Wangeleye's well-known soft and persuasive voice the snake spoke.

"Is it so astonishing, O Djujube, that I should appear in my present disgraceful shape—the shape I bespoke for myself as I lay on my death-bed at Whoopdadoodn?"

"It is more astonishing, O snake, that you should come to trouble us at such a time as this," answered Djujube, speaking civilly to the creature out of respect for its daughter, his wife. "As to your shape, I am very sorry to see it, since it proves that I was wrong in supposing that we were unjustly banished. I will not harm thee, snake, but go away. We will have no dealings with murderers!"

"I am not so particular," replied the snake, regarding Djujube meaningly out of his glistening eyes. "A man may be a murderer fourfold, and if I can help him I will."

Djujube winced. "I know of no fourfold murderers," said he, turning his back to avoid the terribly knowing eyes.

"Nay," answered the snake with an air of indifference, "why should you? Murders are not so rare in these parts that the fact of four men—sacred men and priests—being clubbed in a pit should be known all over the world. Even if one happened to know the murderer it is scarcely likely that he would brag of the acquaintance."

Clearly there was no use in trifling with so well-informed a creature as the snake. "I know now to what you allude, good Wangeleye," said Djujube, facing round, "and very humbly beg pardon if what I said hurt your feelings. But I did not think the case was so bad. I wished merely to send the poor fellows to sleep while I escaped."

"Right, my son; and they are sleeping still," said Wangeleye the snake. "You put them so soundly to sleep that they never woke again. But it was neither to accuse you nor to converse with you on such small matters that I am here."

"How came you to know where we were to be found?" asked Djujube, feeling extremely uncomfortable, and scarcely knowing whether to give his father-in-law the cold shoulder or be friendly with him.

"My daughter, your wife, sent for me."

"How?" exclaimed Djujube in astonishment, and looking from the snake to his wife.

"I did not call him by name!" the still trembling woman exclaimed. "I was so hungry that I prayed that if there was still a lizard or a snake left on the island, be it never so ugly and unfit for food, it would appear to me."

"And hearing her I came," remarked the black snake.

"But not to be eaten," said Djujube.

"No, but to put you in the way of eating—to provide you as long as you choose to stay here with the richest meats and most delicious fruits."

"If that is the purport of your errand, good father-in-law!" exclaimed the young man eagerly, and at the same time he smacked his shrivelled lips with a hungry sound, "we will waste no more time in idle conversation. A brace of well-grown young wild pigs would be exactly the thing just now, with some taro-pudding—eh, wife? eh, my Towsclair? Let us have 'em quick, good Wangeleye!"

"It were as easy as wagging my tail to provide what you ask, and a hundred times as much," the snake answered; "but first of all there is another small matter to arrange. You have in your possession, my son-in-law, the sacred——"

"Hist!" interrupted Djujube, signing to the snake to say not another word.

"The sacred black stone."

"Come a little this way, good snake," whispered the young man from behind his hand; "my wife knows nothing about that terrible thing."

"Yes, indeed, I do, my husband!" cried the woman, cowering to the earth, and trembling in every limb at bare mention of the dread mystery; "my father has told me all."

"Then, since he knows all, what need is there that he should question me?" said Djujube sullenly.

"I know all but where you have hidden it," remarked the snake in a wheedling voice; "it only remains for me to know that, good Djujube, and then all that your heart can desire in the way of eating and drinking shall be yours."

"And of what use would the knowledge where the sacred stone is hidden be to my father-in-law?"

"None to me," replied the snake. "Indeed, it is not on my own account that I am here. I was loath to come, but I was compelled." Here the reptile shuddered, and his tail was seen to quiver.

"Who compelled you?" asked Djujube.

"My master. He wants the sacred black stone."

"Who is your master?"

"The father of snakes—the oldest serpent in the world."

"But can the—what can your master want with the sacred stone?" Djujube asked in a troubled voice; "it can be of no use to him."

"What do *you* want with the useless thing?" asked the snake. "It can be of no service to you; it has served you in no way since you became possessed of it."

"No indeed!" sighed poor Djujube.

"Now you can make it of use," argued the snake persuasively; "you can, by letting me know where it is hidden, make it the means of making yourself and your family fat and prosperous, and that not only for a day, but for all days as long as you live. Think of that!"

But Djujube, who, as before mentioned, was a very shrewd young fellow, shook his head incredulously; said he—

"Since the sacred stone is useless to me, and of no more value in your master's hands, how will he make a good bargain by giving me all you say in exchange for it?"

"Bend down, so that I may whisper in your ear, and I will tell you in what manner my master will make a good bargain," said the snake, winking one of his wicked eyes cunningly.

So Djujube bent down, and the snake whispered a little while in the young man's ear —whispered suggestions so diabolical that his hearer started suddenly to his feet.

"I would sooner die!" cried he wrathfully.

"That were no great sacrifice," sneered the snake, "since you have not a day's life in your starved body. And pray what is your objection? Why should not my master hold the victim stone as well as the priests?"

"Why!" cried the young man in amazement; "are you so simple in your snake shape, O Wangeleye, that you need be told why? Would not your master have all Figi in his hands by to-morrow night if the stone were carried straight to him now?"

"And what will Figi or anything else be to you if you go hungry another day?" demanded the snake. "However, the choice is with you." And he shrugged that part of his sleek body where shoulders grow, as though it was a matter of indifference to him which way his famished son-in-law decided.

"Ay, what will Figi or anything else in the world be to us if we go hungry another day, or another hour even, my husband?" pleaded his famished wife. "What will to-morrow see our child, our dear Towsclair? Would it be nothing, dear Djujube, to behold him again plump and merry as he was on that fatal day when we escaped in the priests' canoes? Would it be nothing for me to see my husband, my brave young warrior, once again hale and handsome? Oh, Djujube, weigh well these advantages, and decide not in haste!"

"Pig! pig and taro pudding!" gasped little Towsclair, who, while nobody was observing him, had devoured the lizard that he and his father had procured after so much trouble.

Poor Djujube was distracted. Hunger, and the feelings of a husband and a father, were wrestling with his better nature, and, alas! the struggle, as might be expected when the contending parties were so unequally matched, was of short duration.

"Tell me, O snake, if I reveal to you the hiding-place of this sacred stone, in how short a time after will the pigs and taro appear?"

"On the instant," replied the snake briskly.

"There will be no delay? You will not require to take the thing to your master before the pigs can be produced?"

"Pigs on delivery," answered the snake in a tone that carried conviction with it.

"Follow me, then," exclaimed Djujube desperately, "and you, wife, while we are gone, make a large fire for roasting, and you, my Towsclair, fetch fresh water to mix the taro."

And so they set off towards that part of the forest that skirted the seashore where

Djujube had concealed the terrible stone; the snake gliding by his side and skipping over fallen trees and mounds with an agility impossible to any creature of the species except one influenced by the Evil One. Once or twice the quick ears of the snake made it fancy that there were footsteps in the neighbourhood, but Djujube assured him that it was impossible.

"Are you sure that you remember the spot where the treasure is concealed?" asked the snake.

"Quite sure. There are three palm-trees standing at right angles, and just in front of them a flat grey stone——"

"Hush!" hissed the snake warningly.

"I was only about to remark that under this flat grey stone we shall find what we are in quest of," whispered Djujube softly.

Not so softly, however, but that the words were overheard. Once again the snake reared his head in a listening attitude, but Djujube assured him that his alarms were groundless.

"We shall soon be there now," said the young man. "When we get to the top of this bank we can see the identical spot."

So they could, and something else as well, as soon as the summit of the steep bank was gained—something that caused the snake's crest to rise ragefully, and his eyes to glare, and his forked tongue to dart and quiver, while as for Djujube, he was dumbfoundered and rooted to the spot in amazement, for lo! there, digging at the spot with its mighty beak and scratching at the flat grey stone with its powerful feet, was the cassowary, the wily and solitary cassowary that the young hunter had endeavoured so frequently and so fruitlessly to subdue.

"Hurry! hurry!" shrieked the snake, "or he'll have it. Load your sling for a cast at the thief, you fool, or he will make off with the precious stone, and yourself and your wife and brat will starve."

And by way of example the snake darted forward, leaving Djujube to follow. But the young man had never thought to bring his sling with him, and even had he it would have availed him nothing, for long ere even the swift snake could reach the spot the cassowary was seen to turn the heavy flat stone completely topsy-turvy, to grope with his beak in the soil beneath for a moment, and then to make off with the speed of the wind. It was as they suspected. When they came up to the hole the black stone and the red

THE BLACK STONE PRIEST RECOVERS THE MAGIC STONE.

feather had vanished. It was curious to witness the wrath of the snake. One moment he stood bolt upright on the tip of his tail, the next he wound himself into curious knots and writhed and wriggled on the shingle, his forked tongue quivering and darting, and his eyes blazing like green fire, while the language he used was something frightful to hear.

"Ruined! ruined! ruined!" it shrieked—"my last chance gone! Doomed for ever and ever! Compelled to return to my terrible dungeon and live in gloom and deep darkness, and all through this chattering fool, who must bellow his secret so that it might be heard a mile off."

"Where was the harm in talking loud when there was nobody to hear?" said Djujube sulkily.

"What harm! this harm," cried the snake: "the 'nobody' that heard is more powerful even than my master. Listen, O most foolish of young men, and learn the truth, since lies nor aught else will help us. This 'nobody' that heard the words so rashly uttered, the 'nobody' whose triumph it was but a moment since to snatch the prize from me when I thought it so sure, is my worst enemy."

"How can so simple a creature as a cassowary be a man's enemy?" asked Djujube in astonishment.

"How can a simple snake talk and understand the language of man, thou dullest of a generation of blockheads?" cried Djujube's father-in-law passionately. "It is no simple cassowary that has outwitted us, it is the 'shape' assumed by the old Black Stone priest for whose murder I am doomed to crawl for ever, as you see me. See what your blundering has done for me. 'Get me this black stone,' said my master, 'that thy son-in-law hath stolen and concealed, and thy reward shall be freedom to live on the earth's surface, instead of its gloomy depths,' and now I must return to whence I came, never more to feel the fresh breeze or know what sunlight is." And the unfortunate snake began to weep piteously.

Djujube was deeply affected. "Be not so downhearted, my father-in-law," said he. "The stone the cassowary has swallowed is a hard and heavy stone, and will, for a time at least, remain undissolved in its gizzard. Procure me, if it is in your power, but one hearty meal to give me strength, and I will sharpen my spear and hunt the bird down. I will chase him as he never yet was chased, and subdue him and regain the treasure, and all may yet be well."

But the snake shook his head despondingly. "I am afraid that my master will be so furious that he will deny the favour you ask, even though it is so small," he replied; "but if you will remain here a little while I will go and inquire."

And so saying the reptile made for a crevice near the root of a tree, and at once disappeared. For a long time Djujube waited, but Wangeleye did not return. Presently, however, he heard a rustling in the bushes, and stepping softly up to see, he there discovered a wild sow with a litter of three squeakers comfortably reposing on the thick grass. To arm himself with the butt-end of a broken bough and deal the pig a fatal blow with it was but the work of a moment, and then catching the squeakers he made a bunch of them by their tails and hurried back to his wife, who by this time had made a great fire. He threw them down without saying a word concerning the unlucky interference of the cassowary, and while they were cooking he went back for the sow, and that too was roasted, and the family sat down to such a dinner as they had not tasted for many a day.

After that Djujube sharpened his spear and set out with the stern determination to overcome the cassowary or perish in the attempt. "I will keep to the skirt of the island," thought the cunning young man, "since the bird will no doubt take to the sea and swim over to Whoopdadoodn. There is no fear of its flying away, its wings are too small and weak."

So he stole softly along the seashore, and after a search of about two hours his quick ears caught the harsh clucking sound the cassowary makes, and, peeping between the trees, there he saw the great bird squatting down and busily engaged in webbing its toes with shreds of fine bark-cord, to enable it the better to swim. So closely had Djujube approached the ingenious creature, that he could have speared it easily had it not been for the intervening thick growth of foliage; but, resolved not to throw away so fair a chance, he looked about him, stealthily taking observations in every direction, and presently spied a bank a little to his right, by crawling to the top of which he would be enabled to overlook his game, and take a strong and fair cast at it.

Immediately he proceeded to put his plan into execution, creeping flat on his belly, and now and then pausing to listen, and to his delight the clucking noise continued, which convinced him that the cassowary was unsuspectingly getting on with its job. He gained the foot of the hill, and, noiseless as a cat, made his way up the side of it until his head was just level with the summit of it. Then he ventured to take a peep, but alas! at the

same moment the cassowary turned his head, and their eyes met, and before Djujube could leap to his feet the agile creature bounded off with a loud cry, and was instantly lost to view.

Luckily, however, and to Djujube's great satisfaction, it turned inland, and not to the sea. "There may yet be a chance: with its toes half webbed it will not be able to run so very fast," and so comforted the young man grasped his spear, and, light as a hare, he sprang away in pursuit. It was as he suspected. The preparations the great bird had made for its sea voyage interfered considerably with its running powers, and ere he had covered a mile of ground, the hunter struck on the spoor of his game freshly indented in the moist earth. This put fresh courage into him, and he sent his long legs spinning over the ground swifter than before, and, turning a corner, there was the cassowary fairly in view.

So great was his delight that, though his life depended on it, he could not refrain from giving vent to a yell of triumph, which the cassowary heard and responded to by a long-sounding and peculiar cry, which Djujube in his ignorance mistook for a cry of despair. But it was not so. The cry the bird uttered was one beseeching help from the good genius of Black Stone, and it was not in vain. Closely and more close did Djujube approach, till at last he was within twenty yards of it, and then he poised his spear for a cast.

But alas! who after this shall doubt the miraculous power of the Black Stone? Fairly enough did the hunter aim his weapon, and throw back his arms to cast it, but, to his dismay, it would not part from him. It adhered to his right hand as though it were nailed there!

Had Djujube been wise he would now have given over the chase as one in which he could by no human possibility succeed; but he was otherwise. Whether it was the effect of the diabolical pork he had eaten is not easy to say; but instead of this manifestation of Black Stone power filling him with awe and humility, it wrought him to raging madness, and with his spear still fixed in his hand he still pursued the cassowary, his feet seeming scarcely to touch the ground.

"Let me lay but a hand on it," gasped the madman; "let me but close my fingers round one of its hateful legs, and we will see how strong Black Stone is to make me loose my hold!"

Infatuated and daring young man! As though to make sport of him, the Black Stone powers allowed him his wish. Gaining on it at every step, and presently springing at the giant bird, he attempted to grasp it by the leg, but in an instant he was sent whirling high up in the air, and down he fell dead as the deadest of those four men he had clubbed in the pit.

That was how his wife and little Towsclair found him, but they saw no more of the cassowary or of the snake. After this, the spell being broken, and the curse of constant famine being removed from the woman and the boy, the birds returned to the island and the remaining animals hiding in holes in terror came out and increased and multiplied, so that when seventeen years after a canoe from Tonga touched at the island by chance, and offered to take off the two solitary inhabitants, they were so perfectly happy that they preferred to stay.

THE CLAY HEAD.

THE WHOOGLES SUCCESSFULLY INVADE THE WILANGS.

THE CLAY HEAD.

Though but a little arm of the sea not more than five miles in width divided them, no two tribes to be found on the whole of the vast Australian tract were so bitterly animated against each other as the Whangs and the Whoggles.

The Whoggles numbered at least ten to one against their enemy, but somehow or another they were repeatedly worsted when it came to blows. The Whangs were so extraordinarily lucky, especially in canoe warfare, and as it was chiefly on the water field that their wrangles and wrongs were referred for settlement, this made it so much the worse for the Whoggles. The canoes of the Whangs were swiftest, and, light though they appeared, a blow of a waddy or ironstone club that would have cracked a Whoggle boat like a nutshell had no more effect on a vessel of the Whang party than though it were flicked with the thumb-nail. If the Whangs cast a boomerang or hurled a spear it was certain to hit its mark as though guided by some invisible agency.

And so it was, though for many years the defeated Whoggles went on wondering and wondering, quite unable to make out the reason why their foes should be attended by such undeviating luck. It was the more annoying since on no account whatever did they deserve it. Though calling themselves Whangs, they were in reality Whoggles as to their origin at least. Many years before, in peaceful times, when the tribe last mentioned was the strongest and most industrious and pacific for miles round, a band of robbers and murderers was discovered amongst them—bloodthirsty and cannibal wretches who made a vow that on the first night of every new moon they would sup off babies' hearts, each monster taking one as his share. To keep up the dreadful supply it was necessary for the members of the band to be on the alert all the month through, roaming through the district, and laying hands on every unguarded child under four years old that fell in their way. They did not slaughter the poor innocents as they caught them; they stored them alive in a great cave down by the seashore, and gave them of the very best to eat and drink, and entertained them with all manner of amusements, in order that they might prove fat and of good flavour when required for the table.

So serious a drain on the Whoggle infantine population could not, of course, continue long unnoticed, and a strict watch was kept to discover the child-stealers. Their final detection was due to a shepherd. Over the great cave where the poor little creatures were stored was a fine bit of pasture, and the man in question used to drive his sheep there when the grass was ripe, that they might get a week or so of rich feeding. He was lying down on the slope one hot afternoon, and thought that he heard his lambs bleating, and knowing that there were wild dogs about, he rose hastily to see; but the lambs were all lying by their dams, quiet and comfortable as could be desired. Once more he lay down, but no sooner had he done so than the bleating sound again made itself heard, and again he rose —to find matters exactly as they were before—but when he once more threw himself down in a pet at being so often disturbed without cause, he again heard the bleating louder than ever.

He was naturally a very thick-headed shepherd, but now his curiosity was fairly roused, and, turning over on his side, he laid his ear to the ground and listened with all his might, and, to his terror and amazement, found that it was not lamb-bleating but baby-crying that he heard. He had with him a long spear, which he carried to keep away the dingos or wild dogs from his flock, and with this he began to dig a hole in the ground; and he dug and dug, the sound of crying each moment becoming more distinct, until presently his spear-point sank through with a suddenness that startled him, and stealthily withdrawing the weapon, he peeped down the hole he had made, and there, in a sort of arched dungeon lit by lamps, with bits of rag for wicks and mutton-fat for oil, he counted seven-and-twenty little children, most of them tumbling and sporting about in all the confiding innocence of childhood with a bellyful, but four or five of them, who had not as yet arrived at that stage of independence which ability to consume solid food confers, were sucking their little thumbs and roaring for their mothers. This was the sound that the shepherd had mistaken for bleating. Busy amongst the little family was an old woman that the shepherd knew very well by sight, and she was nursing the smallest of the squallers, and coaxing it to be quiet, though at the same time she regarded it very savagely. "I wish the new moon were to-morrow, little wretch!" the shepherd heard her mutter, and presently, when his eyes grew more used to the gloom of the cave and enabled him to get a fairer view of the child the old witch was nursing, to his unspeakable rage and astonishment he recognised it to be his own little one that, three weeks ago, being left just outside the wurley (hut) to amuse itself by pulling up worms, had mysteriously disappeared, and never been heard of since. For a moment he was for crying out, and demanding of the old woman how she came by the child, but on second thoughts he saw that he might do better; so he stopped the hole that he had made with a wisp of grass, and fast as his legs would carry him ran back to the village to acquaint the head man with what he had witnessed. He was not unworthy of his distinguished post that head man. "If we make a fuss," said he, "we shall fail to catch anybody but the old woman, and we may be sure that there are more than she concerned in this diabolical business. As for the safety of your own child, shepherd, that need give you no concern, since, as you have seen, it is well looked after, and in no danger until the new moon, as you have heard. It is but three nights to the new moon, and meanwhile you can watch diligently, and we may discover more than we at present suspect."

And even while the two were talking together there came a woman crying and wringing her hands, and complaining that her child was missing. A man had come to beg a drink of water, and while she was fetching it he had caught up her little boy and ran off with it.

"How long since did this happen?" asked the head man, with a glance of intelligence at the shepherd.

"But a few minutes since," replied the weeping woman. "I have run all the way here."

"Run back, then, with all speed," said the head man, "and rest assured that inquiries shall at once be made."

So the woman went off, and soon as they had seen the back of her, said the head man—

"Come along, shepherd! Let us hasten to the hill where your sheep are, and, if we are lucky, by spying down the peephole you speak of we may see something worth our trouble."

So they ran off together, and with little difficulty found the grass plug that stoppered the peephole, and pulled it out, and then, shielding it with his hands that the sun might not shine through (a precaution the stupid shepherd had not taken), the head man spied down, and found matters exactly as the shepherd had described them, except that the shepherd's child was now in good-humour, up to its little eyes in a bowl of wild honey the old woman had set before it. He was about to raise his head and make a comforting remark on the subject to the shepherd, when he heard a sound of tapping down below, and promptly placed his ear at the hole.

H

"Who's there?" the old woman asked.

"Gash-and-gore," was the answer.

"Right; come in."

And, still peeping, the head man saw a door at the end of the cave open and a man come in bearing a child in his arms. He had been running, for he was out of breath.

"There is my new-moon supper, granny," said he; "let me put a mark on it, or some of the rogues will be for palming a half-fed, skinny little wretch on me instead of my own;" and as he spoke he put down his head, and with his sharp white teeth bit out a mouthful of the child's hair.

"Now I shall know it again," said the villain. "Don't let him grow thin, granny; it only wants three days to new moon, you know."

The head man waited to hear no more, but closed the hole, and without a word made his way back with the shepherd to the council-house in the village. Here he called together the elders, and with closed doors imparted to them the strange things that he and the shepherd had witnessed; and after long consultation it was resolved that, since no harm was intended the children until the night of the new moon, no action should be taken till then, but that meanwhile measures should be concocted towards securing the whole fiendish gang, for that one such existed there could be no manner of doubt.

So, letting only men of known probity into the secret, they made arrangements, and by dark of the evening of the new moon a hundred fighting men, well armed, were posted about the hill, while the shepherd and the head man kept watch at the little hole atop. All was dark within, except for a blue light from a great lamp that hung from the ceiling, and which was supplied with kangaroo fat and some oily sort of blue earth, only to be found at the other side of the mountains. There lay all the children on their little beds of dried grass, with nothing particularly noticeable about them, except that under the left breast of each was a broad thick leaf with the edges of it turned up so as to make a rim. The old woman was present too, but she was engaged in a no more remarkable manner than piling sticks and fuel in a hole in the ground, all ready for a great fire.

Presently they that were on the look-out heard a low whistle, and then another and another, and creeping out of the brushwood towards the door of the cave came more than a dozen fellows, all armed and wearing paint, as though they were going to war. Being but new, the moon shed only a feeble light, but to the astonishment of the head man and the

others, there were several amongst the strange band that had hitherto passed as quite respectable characters.

After a friendly greeting, and counting their number, the eldest of the band tapped at the door.

"Who is there?" asked the old woman, as a listener at the hole in the roof could distinctly hear.

"Gash-and-gore."

"Come in."

"Are you ready?"

"Quite. The dishes are there, and the knives are sharp, and the fire is laid," answered the old woman.

"Then we will begin."

So saying he went outside to his companions and told them what the old woman had said, whereon, joining hands gleefully, they immediately engaged in a dance of so diabolical a character, that to see it was enough to make one's blood curdle.

"Now, brethren, we will eat the feast of the new moon," cried the leader, and with that they filed singly into the cave, closing the door after them.

Now not a moment was to be lost. Signalling his forces, the head man stole softly and swiftly to the entry, and tapped at the door in imitation of the tap he had just before heard. The old woman within responded, he gave the password, the door was opened, and in swarmed the guard, overpowering the cannibals instantly, and making every one of them prisoners. By good fortune all the children had escaped injury, though by what a slight hair their lives depended might be judged from the fact that each of the villains, when taken, grasped in his hand one of the short knives the old woman had been sharpening.

And now, had the Whoggles been wise, they would have hung every one of the murderers to a tree, and so an end of them, but, as before observed, they were a most amiable people, and averse to the shedding of blood unnecessarily. They once more called a council, and then it was resolved not to hang so great a batch of criminals, but to banish them with their wives and children to an island about five miles distant, and so give them a chance to reform and repent of their enormities, if they were so inclined.

And did the convicts mend their ways? Not they; they suited them too well. They remained civil while they remained few in number, but there were many growing boys amongst them at the time they were banished, and in four or five years they became men, fearless and ferocious as their fathers. Besides this, by some means they managed to convey to their relatives and acquaintance in the Whoggle country intelligence of what a charming island it was they were living on, and gave such an exaggerated account of it, and of how all the luxuries the world afforded might be there obtained, and not so much as an hour's work in a whole month to pay for it, that a great many of them were induced to desert and come over to the island with their canoes, which the ruffians took mighty good care instantly to destroy, so that all means of getting back might be cut off from them. Then they called themselves Whangs (which can be translated to mean in English nothing else than Satan's horns). Hitherto they had paid tribute to the old country by preparing once a year, to be fetched away by the government canoe, a certain number of spear-heads, stone-hatchets, and boomerangs, but to the complete astonishment of the tax-collectors, one year when they went for their dues, they found all the spears, and hatchets, and boomerangs in the hands of the convicts, instead of neatly tied in bundles, and when they ventured to remonstrate they were assailed with most abominable abuse, and threatened with personal assault if they did not instantly take their departure, at the same time bidding them carry word to their masters that they were no longer to be considered as slaves, that they were now free people, and defied the Whoggles and all creation besides to prove the contrary. Faithfully did the messengers convey an account of the impudent conduct of the Whangs to the head man of the Whoggles, who, confident in the number and bravery of his army, scarcely knew whether to be most amused or vexed at the defiance of the scoundrels. "However, we must let them see that they may not bully us with impunity," said he, and straightway equipped a war-canoe, with a company of picked fighting men, to go over to bring the rioters to their senses, and hang up their ringleader by way of example.

But, as it proved, this order was much more easily given than obeyed. Without the least doubt as to the success of their mission, the Whoggles landed, and seeing a handful of Whang rebels gathered at a little distance, made up to them at once, and demanded to be informed which was their ringleader, so that they might haul him up to a bough at once, and before they proceeded to the execution of the other portion of the unpleasant business with which they were intrusted.

The Whangs were not more than one to two compared with the Whoggles, but to hear the yell of derision that arose from them when the Whoggle officer had concluded his polite speech, one would have thought that the odds were all the other way.

ATROCIOUS RECEPTION OF THE WHOOGLE COMMISSIONERS BY THE WHANGS.

"Come on!" cried the Whangs, flourishing their weapons, "we have no ringleader, being all of a ring, and requiring none."

"Come on, then!" shouted the Whoggle chief officer; "you shall see how we will make your wooden heads ring."

But he had scarcely uttered the word when his own head was put past ringing. A Whang cast a stone from his sling, and, striking it full in the forehead, cracked it irrevocably. Nor was this more than the bare beginning of the Whoggle disasters. Every stone slung from the other side hit its mark, every spear whizzed true as an English arrow, while the weight of their waddies was so tremendous that they came with a clout like the falling of a leaden weight on the heads of the devoted Whoggle soldiery. There was no standing against the murderous onslaught, and, yelling that there was witchery in it all, the few that remained flew to their canoe, and, pushing off hastily, pulled like madmen for the other shore.

And, indeed, there was witchery in it. Along with the other banished wretches was the old woman that used to mind the babies in the cave, and when she was nigh to death she called her kinsmen, and told them that she felt quite convinced that though her spirit was about to leave her body, she should not quit the earth entirely. "I have not the least doubt that from the life I have lived I shall be promoted to be a witch," said she, "and better able to assist you against the rascally Whoggles than I now am."

"That's good!" exclaimed her eldest son, clapping his hands; "make haste and die, that's a good mother!"

"But you must pay me for my services," continued the hag. "What you must do is to get some white clay, and mould an image of my head, and set it up in a wurley, with an old woman to mind it continually, and see that it comes to no harm; and once in every year you must give me two new-born babies. You understand what I mean?"

"We understand, good mother," replied her eldest son, "and you shall be obeyed. Now make haste and die. Why didn't you die before, since you can be of so much more use to us dead than alive?"

"But you will forgive me, my son?" said the old woman faintly; and on his assenting she died happy.

No sooner was the breath out of the old woman's body than her son despatched a messenger for a lump of white clay—the same sort as the Whoggles, and, indeed, all other

Bushmen of Australia, plaster their heads over with as a token of mourning for a deceased friend—and shaped a face and head exactly like hers, and baked it in the fire. Then they built a hut to place it in, and, according to the witch's direction, appointed an old woman to guard it. To mark their sense of the importance of the old woman's duties they allowed her her tobacco and meat, and house and firing; and in case the witch head might require refreshment they doubled the allowance of everything, with strict injunctions to the old woman to set a fair share before her charge three times a day.

But no sooner were they gone than the greedy old woman set to and ate all the meat and smoked all the tobacco. "Did they think I should be such a fool as to let good meat waste before a clay image?" chuckled she. And when the witch's son looked in in the evening to see how his mother's image was, the old woman told him that she was getting along excellently, and was in such good appetite as to consume her fair share of the things that were left, and so much more that she would be glad if for the future the allowance was increased.

And so they increased it, the artful old woman taking the full benefit, and growing so sleek and fat that she was the envy of all the other females of the tribe. But one morning she presented a very different appearance. She looked haggard, and worn, and frightened, and her arms and face bore traces of very recent scratches. Going straight to the wurley where the witch's son lived, she informed him that she was desirous of resigning her office, and when he inquired her reasons for this sudden resolution—for it was only on the evening previous that he had called on her and she had expressed herself as abundantly satisfied—she could only answer that the responsibility was too much for her, and was wearing her out.

"Try it just for another week," urged the witch's son.

"I wouldn't try it for another night, no, not for all the tobacco growing between this and Hayward's Range," answered the old woman shudderingly.

And surely she had good reasons for declining to remain any longer custodian of the terrible head. She was a very cunning old woman, but she had quite overlooked one circumstance, and that was that witches—at least Australian witches—are never so powerful as on the first night of the new moon. She was reminded of the fact in a rather startling manner. As usual, on the evening of the night in question she had gobbled up the double allowance, and then laid down on her mat laughing, as she thought on what a lucky old woman she was, when all of a sudden the new moon was unveiled, and, peeping in at a chink in the thatch, shone on the clay head and awoke it to life. The old woman, huddled in the corner, was like to have expired in fright to see the stony thing roll its eyes and champ its rigid jaws.

"I'm hungry!" moaned the clay head. "Where is the thief that has stolen my meat, and my tobacco, and my honey?"

And, casting about the wurley with its terrible eyes, it presently spied her out, and without more ado slipped off its pedestal and rolled towards her, gnashing its teeth as it rolled. The old woman would have screamed, only that terror locked her mouth, and she could do nothing but skip here and there to avoid the nimble head that so maliciously made at her, all the while snarling like a cat and growling "Twenty days—sixty meals! a bite for every meal at least!" There was no escape from it, for it could bound from one side of the hut to the other as though it were made of indiarubber; and when the old woman bundled herself in her blanket, the head would spy a loose fold and bolt into it quicker than a rat. And so the dishonest old head-minder was mauled and bitten frightfully, until she had received sixty bites—the number of meals she had robbed the witch head of—and then she fainted right away.

In the morning when she roused out of her swoon and opened her eyes there was the clay head perched on its pedestal, and looking as harmless as a baked clay image could, and until the old woman moved she began to think that after all it was only a dream; but when she attempted to rise, and felt such aches in all her bones, and when she examined herself, and discovered the bites and bruises, she no longer had the least doubt, and went and asked permission to give up the situation as already described.

And foreseeing no difficulty in the appointment of a successor, the witch's son, who was the chief of the Whangs, gave her permission, telling her that she was a fool to reject an office that evidently agreed with her so excellently, and one which a hundred women of the tribe would jump for joy to obtain. But somehow or another the story of the old woman's frightful ill-usage had leaked out, and though the most tempting offers were made, no one could be found courageous enough to undertake the office. So, when it came to this, the chief of the Whangs declared that the affairs of the state should not be thrown into confusion because of the whims and fancies of an old woman, and ordered the one that had tendered her resignation to resume her functions without delay. She still objected, but a few applications of stick to her obstinate back made her yield, and she returned to the wurley where the terrible head was, full of the deadliest spite against it, but, nevertheless, disposed to act honestly by it, which was the means of making matters between herself and her charge comparatively comfortable.

Comparatively only. Careful, however, as the old woman might be, she was sure to give occasional offence to the malicious head, and certain as new moon came the time of settling the reckoning. Sometimes she had as many as half-a-dozen bites to endure; at other times, when she had been extra careful, no more than two or three bites and as many bruises; enough, however, to keep alive her spite against the witch, and to set her thinking how she might be revenged on her.

Meanwhile the Whangs began to reap the promised advantage from their possession of the clay image. The first instance of it was in their encounter with the Whoggle officers who came to enforce the taxes, and repeatedly afterwards, in various sea skirmishes and land battles, the presence of the witch's invisible power could not be for a moment doubted. The Whangs acted fairly by their witch. Once in every year, according to their promise, two babies were sacrificed to her, they being chiefly stolen from the Whoggle country by picked robbers of the Whangs. The villains engaged had a tremendously high price paid them for their services, and still more and more as the Whoggles, exasperated by the cases of child-stealing that annually occurred, increased in their vigilance.

At last came a year when the robbers sent to steal the children for the sacrifice returned empty-handed. It was impossible, they declared, to steal even a sly look at a Whoggle baby, let alone the baby itself, since from morning till night the mothers carried their babies tied to them. The worst of it was, still hoping to succeed, they had delayed their return so long that the day after to-morrow, as it were, was the appointed time of sacrifice, and here they were without victims.

There was no help for it; since Whoggle babies could not be procured, Whang babies must be substituted.

Now it so happened that the granddaughter of the old woman who still kept the clay head had a month or so before given birth to two boys. They were beautiful little fellows, and sore indeed was their mother's heart when she heard the dismal news, fearing that one of her darlings would be snatched away from her. But even her worst fears only came to within half-way of the dreadful pangs to which she was condemned. The chief of the Whangs sent her word that he had considered the matter, and had decided that both her babies would be wanted. "It were a pity," he said, "to impose on her the painful task of choosing which child she would give up, and he had resolved to spare her the distressing ordeal by taking both."

The edict of the chief was law, and there was no appeal from it. So the young woman went weeping to her grandmother, the keeper of the clay head, and told her the pitiful story. The old woman's wrath and indignation was beyond expression. Reckless of the penalty she would certainly have to pay come the time of new moon, she abused the clay head and reviled it as the prime cause of all her misery, and presently worked her wrath to such a high pitch that she punched the head, so that it rolled off its perch on to the ground, and its nose was broken off.

"Now you have made bad worse, grandmother, since my babies will not be saved, and when they see how you have served the head, you will be punished."

"I don't care," cried the grandmother. "I am too old to care even if they take my life away; but there is no great harm done: we will soon stick the nose on again, and nobody will be the wiser."

So she ran out into the forest and scraped a bit of gum off a tree, and brought it back, and tried to stick the nose on again; and since it stuck in its place, she thought she had succeeded.

"Ah-hah! you wicked witch," cried the old woman exultingly; "you may bite and bruise me when your time comes, but your ugly nose will not tell tales."

But it would have been better had she restrained her feelings, at least until the gum set, for even as she spoke the nose slipped slowly down over the upper lip of the clay face till it rested on the lower, and then, quick as a flash of lightning, the clay mouth opened and shut again, and the nose was swallowed. After which extraordinary and startling performance the head assumed its former stoniness and senselessness.

Here, now, was a frightful condition of things. To have discovered the image of his mother with a damaged nose would have been bad enough, but when the chief found that feature vanished entirely, what would he say? No lie that could be invented would account for the deficiency, and the truth would appear more ridiculous than the most barefaced of lies.

"I'd smash it up altogether," cried the desperate old woman, "and say that it had disappeared, I knew not where, in the night, only they would be sure to trace the remains of it."

"Throw it into the sea," suggested the granddaughter; "there it will be drowned, and you will hear no more of it."

"You forget, child, that it is a witch, and, clay though it is, would swim like a fish," returned the old woman. So she covered her face with her hands and sat by the fire thinking, and presently she jumped up, and going to the cupboard where fat for the lamp was kept, took it out, together with some flour, and began making dough as fast as she was able.

"Pray what are you doing, grandmother?" asked the young woman. "I have had my supper."

"This is not for you, my child," replied the other, shaking her head and winking, to convey to her granddaughter that there was more in the wind than she could then conveniently explain. "This is supper for my charge; it is not yet her time, but I can judge how hungry she must be by her swallowing her nose in so ravenous a manner."

So the granddaughter said no more, and the old woman went on with her dough, putting plenty of fat in it, and spreading it out with her hands. When she had mixed it sufficiently she took it up and suddenly threw it over the witch head, enveloping it completely, so that it appeared like a great pudding. Then she went to the cupboard again and got some slate-coloured powder that smelt something like cinnamon, and this she sprinkled over the dough ball.

"Why, grandmother, you are not going fishing?" exclaimed the young woman. "That is the powder the fishers use to entice their game."

"Come along with me and I will show you," replied the old woman; and with that she took the head and hid it under her cloak, and they went out together.

It was by this time quite dark, and they took their way towards the beach and kept along it for a mile or more until they came to a very wild part of it—a part generally avoided by the bathers, because of the number of sharks known to swarm just at that spot. Here the old woman halted, and taking the head from under her cloak, cast it into the sea, and scarcely had it touched the surface when the snout of a shark was seen to rise and snap at it, and in a moment shark and head vanished.

"Now we shall see if the wicked witch, the devourer of little children, is stronger than a shark!" cried the old woman. So they returned the way they came by the beach, until they reached the place where the canoes were stranded.

"Help me, quick, to launch this small one," said the old woman; "and you take your two babies and paddle over to the Whoggle shore, and tell the people there that

they need no longer fear the Whaugs, for their idol is drowned and all their courage is dead with it."

"And what will you do, grandmother?" asked the young woman; "will you not come with me?"

"No; I will stay and pretend that the head is vanished, I know not how."

So, although very reluctant to leave her good grandmother behind, the young woman did as the other bade, and took her two babies, and paddled with such a will that in two hours she was landed on the opposite island.

As for the old woman, she hurried back as soon as she could; but, to her dismay, as she put her head inside her hut, who should be striding impatiently to and fro within but the witch's son.

"Where is my mother?" he demanded.

"Ah, where!" answered the old woman, rapidly recovering her presence of mind. "I have just returned from seeking her."

"What was the occasion of her going out at this time of night?" said he.

"There was a noise as of babies crying outside, and all at once the head rolled down and out at the door, and that was the last that I saw of it."

"Ah! and how long since is that?" asked the chief, his brow lowering and his eyes gathering full of suspicion.

"About an hour."

"Since dark, then?"

"Since dark."

"And how came thy door open after dark? Traitor, you have attempted to get rid of my mother's image because you had grown sick of the task of tending it!" And so saying, he leaped to his feet and dealt the poor old woman such a violent blow with his waddy that she died on the spot.

Then he went outside and spread the doleful news that their guardian spirit, the fountain-head of their courage, was gone, and that unless she returned nothing but ruin was before them. And when they heard this, with dismal yells they joined hands and danced the lamentation dance, striking themselves and each other with their clubs and spears, and tearing their hair, and calling on the clay head and imploring it to make haste and return to them.

Meanwhile the woman with her two children made her way to the Whoggle village, and knocking up the head man, told him her story. But he did not seem disposed to believe in it.

"And why did not your grandmother come in the boat with you?" he demanded.

"It was only a little one we could launch between us," replied the woman. "There was not room in it for her."

"You act the part very well indeed," said he knowingly; "but we are much too old to be taken in. What fools we should look if we were snared over to the accursed Whang shore and butchered as they have before butchered us!" So he called up the guard. "Bind this woman," said he, "and to-morrow morning we will settle the manner of death she shall die." And they bound her and thrust her into a strong hut with her babies.

And without doubt, for her story was but a lame one, she would have suffered as promised, and left her little ones motherless, had not something very wonderful happened early next morning. As some fishermen were looking after the traps they had overnight set to catch crabs, about half-a-mile from the shore they spied a tremendous fish leaping out of the water, and beating about and whirling rapidly round in a manner such as they had never before seen in fish, big or little. Gradually the monster approached the shore, and then they made it out to be a shark. Evidently it had been fatally wounded or was seriously ill, for it lay on its back gasping for breath in a very pitiful way.

Seeing it so helpless, one fisherman bolder than the rest lashed a great hook to a strong line, and swimming out till he came within ten yards of the shark, threw out his hook, and so fairly, that it at once stuck in the gills of the giant fish, and then he made for the shore, towing his prize by the line. When the creature neared the beach it seemed suddenly to rouse to a sense of its danger, and floundered and plunged madly. But it was now too late. Four sturdy fellows were hauling at it with a will, while a fifth, standing on the strand, contributed to the abatement of its struggles by casting spears at its most vital parts.

Such a prize as a shark seldom fell to the Whoggles, who were but indifferent fishermen, and the outcry they made as they dragged their game into the village was deafening. It was such a tremendous weight that they could not drag it very far, but everybody in the village had heard the din—including the head man—and came running to see. They were indeed amazed. It was extraordinary enough that five men should land a shark of such monstrous proportions at all; but that a shark, seemingly in the full vigour of life, and

The Living Tomb of the Clay Head is Brought on Shore.

with nothing the matter with it, should allow itself to be so easily captured seemed more wonderful than all.

"Except where the spears struck, it is as sound a fish as ever swam," exclaimed one.

"It is a young shark, too; you can tell that by the curl of his tail and the whiteness and soundness of his teeth," said another, "so he couldn't have come by his death through old age."

"But what is that lump projecting just at the pit of the stomach?" asked a third.

"What indeed?" As the fellow spoke, the head man too observed the strange-looking protuberance, and a suspicion of the true state of the case instantly flashed to his mind.

"Bring me a hatchet," said he.

And they brought him a hatchet, and he made a slash at the spot where the lump was, and, as if by magic, out rolled the clay head, the dough by this time all worn off, and exposing the features of the old woman who had kept the babies in the cave unmistakably, in spite of her broken nose.

Even before the head man spoke a word the mob gathered about, recognised the face, and cried out in their astonishment. Then the head man up and told them the story the young woman that had come over last night from Whang had related to him. In a body they rushed to the hut where the poor thing lay trembling with her two little boys, past all hope of life, and only wondering what the manner of her death would be. Even when with joyful shouts they hurried her out, she did not know but that they were about to lead her to the place of execution; and it was only when they arrived at the spot where the dead shark lay and where the head man still stood with the clay head in his hands, exhibiting it to stragglers as they came hurrying up from the far end of the village to inquire what such a tremendous row was about, that she began to have an inkling of the exact state of the case.

When she saw the shark and the head her terror gave way to gratitude, and, sinking down on her knees, being a heathen, and knowing not what else should be done, she kissed the grisly lips of the sea monster, and laughed and cried over it. It was clear now to the head man, to the woman, to everybody, how the seeming miracle had been brought about. The clay head, taken into the shark's stomach, had caused it a mortal fit of indigestion, in the pangs of which it had floundered to the Whoggle shore, and there was captured as has been shown.

Now indeed could there no longer be a doubt as to the truth of the story the woman had told, and, since the abominable Whangs had lost the pluck the presence of their idol gave them, the sooner they were attacked the better, otherwise they might be making another head or something of the kind, and so secure a renewal of their lease of valour. To this effect the head man harangued the people about him, and with one voice they declared that he spoke well.

Straightway the war canoes were manned and launched, the head man himself taking his place in the foremost one, and by voice and gesture encouraging the others, who as they neared the field of action kept considerably astern, and paddled with much less energy than at starting.

But there was no cause for fear or hesitation in approaching the once terrible Whang island. High and low the bereaved savages sought the precious head, offering incredible wealth as a reward for its recovery, but, of course, all to no purpose. When they discovered that the woman with her two doomed babies had disappeared, it occurred to them that perhaps she had fled with them, and the head, fearing their escape, had bowled after them in pursuit, and, by way of enticing it back, it was resolved to sacrifice three other children. The woman missing had three other children, all very young, though not exactly babies, so, in spite of the distracted father's tears and entreaties, these were seized on and ruthlessly slain and laid before the pedestal on which the head used to stand; and in addition to this, and by way of still further pleasing the witch, it was futher resolved that the escaped woman's husband (who, by-the-bye, was a Whang only by compulsion, having been beguiled from Whoggleland in the artful manner previously intimated) should be sacrificed, too, by burning at the stake.

And the three little children were sacrificed as designed, but, as it happened, the crowning atrocity, the murder of their father, was not consummated. The opportune landing of the Whoggles prevented it. Indeed, so intent was the whole population on the contemplated sacrifice, and in building a pyre for the victim and arranging him conveniently atop of it, that they did not even perceive the landing of the enemy, nor, indeed, know anything of the invasion until the doughty Whoggles burst from their ambush, and with the cries of conquerors surrounded the wretches who for so many years had harassed and insulted them. Just as they had struck up the chant of sacrifice and were about to apply the torch to the pyre the interference took place, and the victim released instantly seized a spear, and fought on the side of the Whoggles with the strength and ferocity of three men.

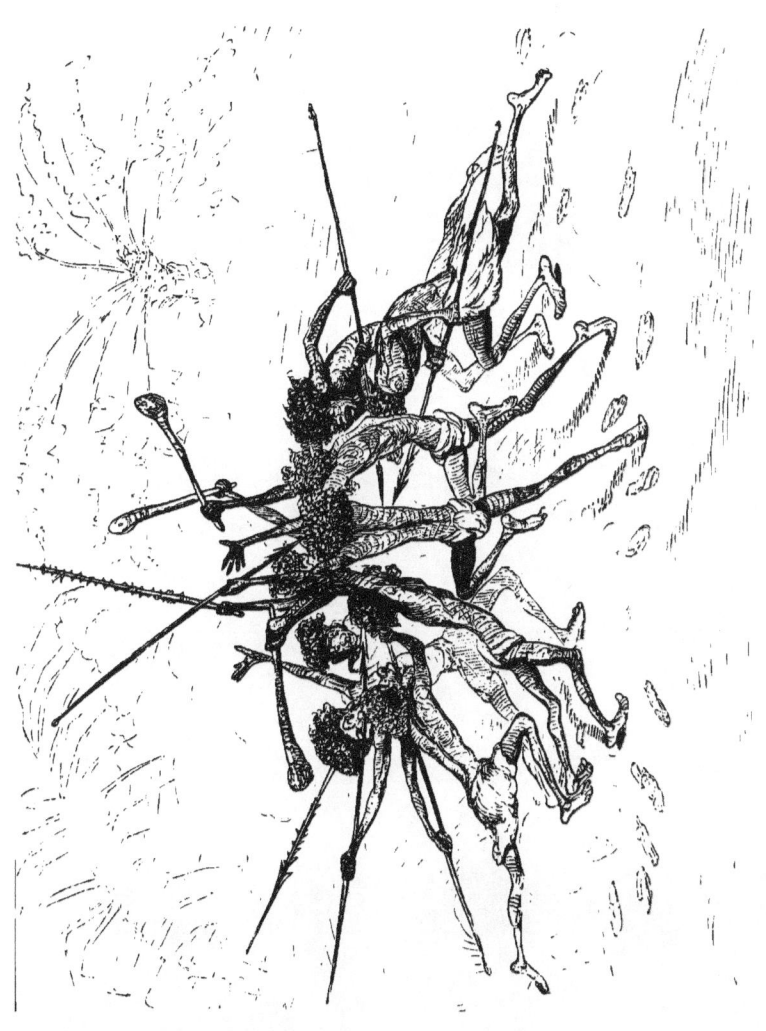

The fight, however, was of but brief duration. The Whangs were panic-stricken, and finding themselves hemmed in on every side threw down their arms like cowards, as they were, and implored mercy. For the very first time in all their lives the Whoggles sternly refused it. Child stealers and murderers to a man they were all worthy of instant death, and that was their doom; some by the club, some by the spear, and the remainder by hanging. In all respects but one was the triumph complete. On overhauling the slain there were missing the witch's eldest son, the leader of the Whangs, and his two nephews, both villains of the deepest dye, inferior only to their uncle in every species of wickedness.

Still, however, it *was* a triumph—a complete and unexpected victory—and as such it was celebrated. That very evening a great feast was made, at which there were fruits of all kinds and meats of——

Well, we will say nothing as to the meat. It is true that there *were* afterwards found several heaps of bones that were not those of sheep or kangaroo, and it is likewise undeniable that a conquering army will at times be guilty of excesses it would blush to confess to afterwards; but then, on the other hand, the Whoggles were a people most simple in their diet, and had always set their faces in the most determined manner against can——

However, it is an unpleasant subject, and perhaps the least said about it the better under any circumstances.

Let the feast be of whatever character it might, there was one man who did not partake of it. This was the father of the three children whom the Whang chief had so barbarously sacrificed—the man who himself so narrowly escaped a cruel and painful death. He it was who was most diligent in hunting amongst the slain; he it was who was the first to proclaim the witch's son and his nephews missing. While the others sat down to eat and drink and make merry, he, after selecting a choice spear, stole off, bound on a mission of vengeance.

And by-and-by, when the feast was over, there was an outcry about the victim the Whoggles had rescued from the fire, and who had not been seen since the commencement of the feast. What had become of him?

"Perhaps he is afraid that, being a Whang, or at least found in Whang company, his life is forfeited," said the head man, "but we all too well remember how well he fought for us to hurt him; let him be sought and brought before me."

164   THE CLAY HEAD.

So they sought him that night, and the next day, and the next, and about noon of the third day they found him as will be seen below. It was not a pleasant picture to contemplate, but without doubt it was a supremely satisfactory one to the father of the sacrificed babies. His vengeance was complete. The middle head, stuck up for his contemplation, was that of the witch's eldest son, while right and left was the head of a nephew.

And there the terrible relics were left, stuck up just as they were, as spoil for the crows and vultures that speedily took up their quarters on the abandoned island of the evil name.

FINAL APPEARANCE OF THE HEADS OF THIS TALE.

Printed by Jas. Wade, 18, Tavistock-street, Covent-garden, London.

POPULAR AND INTERESTING BOOKS

PUBLISHED BY

JOHN CAMDEN HOTTEN.

This day, in 2 vols., 8vo, very handsomely printed, price 16s.,

THE HOUSEHOLD STORIES OF ENGLAND.

POPULAR ROMANCES
OF
THE WEST OF ENGLAND;
OR, THE
DROLLS OF OLD CORNWALL.
COLLECTED and EDITED by ROBERT HUNT, F.R.S.

ILLUSTRATED BY GEORGE CRUIKSHANK.

*** *For an Analysis of this important work see printed description, which may be obtained gratis at the Publisher's.*

The Work is in Two Series. The *First* embraces the FABULOUS AGE, or PRE-HISTORIC PERIOD; the *Second*, THE ROMANCES AND SUPERSTITIONS OF HISTORIC TIMES. Many of these Stories are remarkable for their wild poetic beauty; others surprise us by their quaintness; whilst others, again, show forth a tragic force which can only be associated with those rude ages which existed long before the period of authentic history.

OPINIONS OF THE PRESS.

" Mr. Hunt has done excellent service in collecting all the Cornish Legends he could gather from wide and scattered s urces. In folk-lore this book is rich, and the illustrations have much peculiarity and novelty in them. In them and in the legends generally there is much matter for thought."—*Athenæum.*

" The tales are of the most varied kind; some are particularly interesting, and few have as yet appeared in print. We can recommend them to our readers all the more cordially because we entirely concur with Mr. Hunt, that stories like these have a great historical value."—*Reader.*

" The work is altogether one of the best of the sort we have ever seen."—*London Review.*

John Camden Hotten 74 and 75, Piccadilly, W.

BOOKS READY AND IN PREPARATION.

This day, pp. 323, in 8vo, price 6s. 6d., by post 7s.,
NEW DICTIONARY OF COLLOQUIAL ENGLISH.

SLANG DICTIONARY;
OR,
The Vulgar Words, Street Phrases, and "Fast"
Expressions of High and Low Society;

Many with their Etymology, and a few with their History traced.

WITH CURIOUS ILLUSTRATIONS.

Egyptian Hieroglyphic verb, to be drunk, showing the amputation of a man's leg. See under BREAKY LEG (viz. *Strong Drink*) in the Dictionary, p. 81.

Hedge and Wooden Spoon. See p. 273.

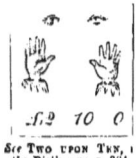

See TWO UPON TEN, the Dictionary, p. 261.

** With this work is incorporated *The Dictionary of Modern Slang, Cant, and Vulgar Words*, issued by "a London Antiquary" in 1859. The first edition of that work contained about 3000 words; the second, issued twelve months later, gave upwards of 5000. Both editions were reviewed by the critical press with an approval seldom accorded to small works of the kind. During the four years that have elapsed, the compiler has gone over the field of unrecognised English once more. The entire subject has been resurveyed, out-lying terms and phrases have been brought in, new street-words have been added, and better illustrations of old colloquial expressions given. The result is the volume before the reader, which offers, for his amusement or instruction, nearly 10,000 words and phrases commonly deemed "vulgar," but which are used by the highest and lowest, the best, the wisest, as well as the worst and most ignorant of society.

John Camden Hotten, 74 and 75, Piccadilly, W.

This day, on toned paper, cloth, price 3s. 6d., by post 3s. 10d.,
ARTEMUS WARD'S NEW BOOK
AMONG THE MORMONS.

Edited by E. P. HINGSTON, Agent and Companion to ARTEMUS WARD whilst "on the Rampage."

John Camden Hotten, 74 and 75, Piccadilly.

Curious Books, Worth Having.

(See *The Times*, Jan. 22nd.)

Army Lists of Charles I. and O. Cromwell, 1642. 7s. 6d.

Satirical Notices of the "Long Parliament," with List, 1645. 7s. 6d.

Magna Charta, Fac-simile of Original, emblazoned in gold and colours. 5s.

Roll of Battle Abbey. Arms emblazoned in gold and colours. 5s.

Warrants to Execute Chas. I. and Mary Queen of Scots. 2s. each.

Dictionary of Oldest Words in the English Language. 2s. 6d.

Foster (or Forster) Family, the History of. 12s. 6d.

Common Prayer. Beautifully Illustrated by Holbein, &c. 10s. 6d.

Family and County History. Catalogue of 2,0000 books, &c. 5s.

Joe Miller's Jests. The genuine original. 9s. 6d.

Catalogue of Curious and Interesting Books. Gratis.

Dictionary of American Slang. By Bartlett. Pp. 550. 12s. 6d.

Roll of Carlaverock. Earliest heraldic work known. 140 Arms emblazoned in gold and colours. A beautiful book. 18s.

Order direct from the Publisher, John Camden Hotten, Piccadilly, London.

This day, in 8vo, handsomely printed, price 12s. 6d.

DIAMONDS AND PRECIOUS STONES;
THEIR HISTORY, VALUE, AND PROPERTIES.
WITH SIMPLE TESTS FOR ASCERTAINING THEIR REALITY.
By H. EMANUEL, F.R.G.S.
With numerous Illustrations, coloured and plain.

☞ Although this Work is intended as a plain and practical Guide to Buyers and Sellers of Precious Stones, the History and Literature of the subject have not been overlooked. Anecdotes of the peculiar accidents and strange fortune which have attended some Jewels are given, and what is hoped will be found a valuable Bibliography of the subject is added as an Appendix at the end.

AN EXTRAORDINARY BOOK.
Beautifully printed, thick 8vo, new half Morocco, Roxburghe style, 12s. 6d.

CONTES DROLATIQUES
(DROLL TALES COLLECTED FROM THE ABBEYS OF LORAINE).
By BALZAC.
With Four Hundred and Twenty-Five Marvellous, Extravagant, and Fantastic Woodcuts by GUSTAVE DORÉ.

₊ The most singular designs ever attempted by any artist. This book is a fund of amusement. So crammed is it with pictures that even the *fainéants* are adorned with thirty-three Illustrations. Now the reader is made to smile at the mishaps of some fat monks; then a battle scene, with fighting men jammed in inextricable confusion until the picture becomes painful to look at, occupies his attention; next, some portraits of fellows who would pass for Pluto's firemen, all seared, as though they had been for a thousand years stirring molten lava; then knights making love, and kissing through their visors; then dreamy old German cities, with diablerie, or sainswills, going on right and left—but all so quaint, so wonderful, that the beholder confesses he never looked upon the like before.

John Camden Hotten, 74 and 75, Piccadilly.

☞ *The Reader is requested to note the following announcements of New and Interesting Books:—*

THE

HISTORY OF SIGNBOARDS,

FROM THE

EARLIEST TIMES TO THE PRESENT DAY.

With ANECDOTES of FAMOUS TAVERNS, REMARKABLE
CHARACTERS, Ancient MARTS of BUSINESS,
COFFEE and other OLD HOUSES in the
large and small Towns up and
down the Country.

By JACOB LARWOOD, assisted by JOHN CAMDEN HOTTEN.

☞ Nearly 100 most curious Illustrations on Wood are given, showing the various old Signs which were formerly hung from Taverns and other houses.

John Camden Hotten, 74 and 75, Piccadilly W.

BOOKS READY AND IN PREPARATION.

ORIGINAL AND ONLY COMPLETE ENGLISH EDITION.
This day, POPULAR EDITION, price 1s., by post 1s. 2d.,
THE CHOICEST HUMOROUS POETRY OF THE AGE.

THE BIGLOW PAPERS,
BY JAMES RUSSELL LOWELL.

*** THE ONLY CORRECT EDITION, WITH NOTES FOR THE ENGLISH READER.

The Times of 25th July, 1864, says:—"To associate the names of eminent persons with ludicrous images * * * keen and caustic political satire. America has produced an excellent specimen of this kind of writing in the celebrated *Biglow Papers* of Mr. Lowell."

The work has frequently been alluded to in the House of Commons, and is acknowledged by the most fastidious of our English critics, to be the keenest piece of satire and the best humorous poetry of the present century.

John Camden Hotten, 74 and 75, Piccadilly, W.

USEFUL AND SCIENTIFIC BOOKS.

Now ready, SECOND EDITION, in binding ornamented with postage stamps, price 1s., by stamps, post 1s. 2d.

POSTAGE-STAMP COLLECTING,
A Standard Guide to;
Or a Complete List of all the Postage Stamps known to exist, with their Values and Degrees of Rarity.

BY MESSRS. BELLARS AND DAVIE.

☞ This SECOND EDITION gives upwards of 300 Stamps not in the previous issue.

"A new Handbook is about to appear, with the title, '*The Standard Guide to Postage-Stamp Collecting, with their Values and Degrees of Rarity,*' a work upon which the authors, Messrs. Bellars and Davie, have been engaged for three years. It will include an account of the Mormon Stamp issued by Brigham Young in 1852."—*London Review.*

"Unexceptionable in the quality of the paper, clearness of print, &c., it affords an addition to the scientific knowledge attainable by means of the study of postage stamps. A table of characters affords the possessor an opportunity of obtaining an acquaintance with the shape and comparative rarity of stamps. This insight into the marketable value and scarcity of postage stamps is a new feature in books on the subject. The exact words of the inscription on the stamps is greatly conducive to facility of identification, and the queer characters on the Moldavian, Russian, &c., stamps, copied without error, demonstrate the extreme care with which the work must have been got up. The index and money table appended will be found very convenient."—*The Stamp Collectors' Magazine.*

THE STANDARD WORK ON CONFECTIONERY AND DESSERTS, USED IN HER MAJESTY'S HOUSEHOLD.

Now ready, SECOND EDITION, with numerous Illustrations, price 6s. 6d., by post 7s.

THE MODERN CONFECTIONER:
A Practical Guide to the latest and most improved Methods for Making the Various Kinds of Confectionery;
With the Manner of Preparing and Laying out Desserts; adapted for Private Families or Large Establishments.

BY WILLIAM JEANES,

Chief Confectioner at Messrs. Gunters' (Confectioners to Her Majesty), Berkeley-square.

*** A new and reliable work on the making of Confectionery and the laying out of Desserts has long been wanted. No pains have been spared to make the present book a useful and safe guide to all Cooks and Housekeepers in private families or large establishments. The name of the chief confectioner at the justly-celebrated house of Gunter & Co., in Berkeley-square, is a sufficient guarantee of the usefulness of the book.

"The most important work which has been published for many years upon the art of making Confectionery, Pastry, and on the arrangement and general ordering of Desserts."—*Daily News.*

"The language is so simple that a child can with ease understand the longest recipes."—*Observer.*

"All housekeepers should have it."—*Daily Telegraph.*

John Camden Hotten, 74 and 75, Piccadilly, W.

This day, on toned paper, price 3s. 6d. ; by post 3s. 10d.
ORPHEUS C. KERR

[OFFICE SEEKER]
PAPERS.
Edited by E. P. Hingston, Agent and Companion to Artemus Ward whilst on the Rampage.

John Camden Hotten, 74 and 75, Piccadilly, W.

HISTORY OF PLAYING CARDS,

This day, choicely printed, pp. 600, price 7s. 6d.,

History of Playing Cards, with Anecdotes of their
Uses in ANCIENT and MODERN GAMES, CONJURING FORTUNE-TELLING, and CARD-SHARPING. Illustrated with Sixty Curious Woodcuts on tinted paper.

Specimen Illustration.

WITH ANECDOTES OF

Skill and Sleight of Hand.	Card Revels and Blind Hookey.
Gambling and Calculation.	Picquet and Vingt-et-un.
Cartomancy and Cheating.	Whist and Cribbage.
Old Games and Gaming Houses.	Old Fashioned Tricks.

John Camden Hotten, 74 and 75, Piccadilly, W.

BOOKS READY AND IN PREPARATION.

Now ready, 4to, beautifully printed, in handsome binding, price 7s. 6d.

DOGS IN THE OLDEN TIME.

VARIETIES OF DOGS,
AS THEY ARE FOUND IN OLD SCULPTURES, PICTURES, ENGRAVINGS, AND BOOKS.

With the names of the Artists by whom they are represented, showing how long many of the numerous Breeds now existing have been known.

By Ph. CHARLES BERJEAU.

. The volume forms a handsome small 4to, is printed on tinted paper, and contains numerous admirable facsimiles by Mr. Berjeau. Some of the dogs, from the engravings by Albert Durer, are the veritable Scotch terriers of Leech, so familiar to all readers of *Punch*. The book is a most pleasing and satisfactory combination of modern and antiquarian interest. The regular price of the book is 10s. 6d., but Mr. Hotten can sell a copy for 7s. 6d.

John Camden Hotten, 74 and 75, Piccadilly, W.

AUTHORISED AND ONLY COMPLETE EDITION.
New Edition, This day, price 1s. ; by post, 1s. 2d.

ARTEMUS WARD,
HIS BOOK.

New Shilling Edition, containing the whole of the Original, with EXTRA CHAPTERS supplied by the Author. One of the most mirth-provoking volumes ever published.

The following are the EXTRA CHAPTERS in Mr. Hotten's NEW and ONLY COMPLETE EDITION, every copy of which will bear the Author's Signature:—

Babes in the Wood.	A. Ward's First Umbrella.
Tavern Accommodation.	Brigham Young's Wives.
Betsy-Jain Re-Orgunized.	Mormon Bill of Faro.

Artemus Ward's Brother.

"He is as clever as Thackeray in Jeames's Dialogue and Policeman X's ballads. There is no merriment in him; it is all dry, sparkling humour."—SPECTATOR.

John Camden Hotten, 74 and 75, Piccadilly, W.

This day, 4th Edition, on tinted paper, bound in cloth, neat, price
3s. 6d. ; by post, 3s. 10d.

NOTICE.—ARTEMUS WARD.

The "Author's Edition ;" containing, in addition to the above, two
extra chapters, entitled, "THE DRAFT IN BALDINSVILLE, WITH MR.
WARD'S PRIVATE OPINION CONCERNING BACHELORS," and "MR. W.'S
VISIT TO A GRAFFICK" [Soirée].

"We never, not even in the pages of our best humourists, read anything so laughable
and so shrewd as we have seen in this book by the mirthful Artemus."—*Public Opinion*.

Now ready, on toned paper, handsomely printed, price 1s. 6d.

A SENSATION IN SEVERAL PAROXYSMS.

BY

THOMAS HOOD.

IDIOTICALLY ILLUSTRATED BY

WILLIAM BRUNTON.

☞ One of the most amusing volumes which have been published for
a long time. For a piece of broad humour, of the highly sensational
kind, it is perhaps the best effort of Mr. Hood's pen.

John Camden Hotten, 74 and 75, Piccadilly, W.

AN ENTIRELY NEW BOOK OF DELIGHTFUL FAIRY TALES.
Handsomely printed, on toned paper, in cloth green and gold, price
4s. 6d. plain,—5s. 6d. coloured (by post 6d. extra),

Family Fairy Tales; or, Glimpses of Elfland at
Heatherston Hall. Edited by PENNELL, Author of "Puck on
Pegasus," &c.; adorned with BEAUTIFUL PICTURES of "MY LORD
LION," "KING UGGERMUGGER," and other great folks.

CONTENTS:

My Lord Lion.	The Great Forest.
The Blue Fish.	The Legend of the Little Flower.
King Uggermugger; or, The Princess Silver-Silk.	"Patch;" or, The Smile Fairy. The Story of the Spring Fairies.
See Me. Spider Face.	A Fable with a Moral.

*** This charming volume of Original Tales has been
universally praised by the critical press.

"A store of droll fancies and pretty thoughts."—*Athenæum*.
"They fully deserve the care which has preserved them, and in their present dress
will afford great amusement at the fireside. The collection is excellent; the illustrations good."—*London Review*.
"The tales are of the most charming kind we have read for a long time. Our author
is as tender as he is quaint and humourous. The illustrations have our heartiest admiration. Miss Edwards works with a pencil as graceful as it is facile."—*Reader*.

See Specimen Illustration on opposite page.

Now ready, 8vo, with numerous Illustrations, price 6s. 6d.,

Gunter's Modern Confectioner: a Practical Guide
to the latest and most improved methods for making the various kinds
of Confectionery; with the manner of Preparing and Laying-out
Desserts; adapted for Private Families or large Establishments.

"The most important work which has been published for many years upon the art
of making Confectionery, Pastry, and on the arrangement and general ordering of
Desserts."—*Daily News*.

Now ready, in post 8vo, beautifully printed, price 7s. 6d.,

Thackeray: the Humourist and the Man of Letters.
The Story of his Life and Literary Labours. With some particulars
of his Early Career never before made public. By THEODORE
TAYLOR, Esq., Membre de la Société des Gens de Lettres.
Illustrated with a PHOTOGRAPHIC PORTRAIT and other Illustrations,
and INCLUDES ANECDOTES of the London Literati, &c.

This day, choicely printed, pp. 600, price 7s. 6d.,

History of Playing Cards, with Anecdotes of their
USES in ANCIENT and MODERN GAMES, CONJURING, FORTUNE-
TELLING, and CARD-SHARPING. Illustrated with Sixty Curious
Woodcuts on tinted paper.

WITH ANECDOTES OF

Skill and Sleight of Hand.	Card Revels and Blind Hookey.
Gambling and Calculation.	Picquet and Vingt-et-un.
Cartomancy and Cheating.	Whist and Cribbage.
Old Games and Gaming Houses.	Old Fashioned Tricks.

John Camden Hotten, 74 and 75, Piccadilly, W.

FAMILY FAIRY TALES.

LEGEND OF THE LITTLE FLOWER.—(*See opposite page.*)

BOOKS READY AND IN PREPARATION.

This day, on toned paper, price 6d.,

Robson; a Sketch, by George Augustus Sala.
An interesting Biography of the great Serio-Comic Actor, with Sketches of his famous Characters, "Jem Baggs," "Boots at the Swan," "The Yellow Dwarf," "Daddy Hardacre," &c. *Anecdotes of the old Olympic Theatre are also given.*

Now ready, NEW AND POPULAR EDITION, post 8vo, pp. 336, price 2s.,

Anecdotes of the Green Room and Stage; or,
Leaves from an Actor's Note-Book, at Home and Abroad. By GEORGE VANDENHOFF.

Mr. Vandenhoff, who earned for himself, both in the Old and New Worlds, the title of the CLASSIC ACTOR, has retired from the Stage. His reminiscences are extremely interesting, and include Original Anecdotes of the Keans (father and son), the two Kembles, Macready, Cooke, Liston, Farren, Elliston, Braham and his Sons, Phelps, Buckstone, Webster, Chas. Mathews; Siddons, Vestris, Helen Faucit, Mrs. Nisbett, Miss Cushman, Miss O'Neil, Mrs. Glover, Mrs. Chas. Kean, Rachel, Ristori, and many other dramatic celebrities.

Now ready, handsomely printed, price 1s. 6d., cloth, gilt edges, 2s. 6d.,

Hints on Hats, adapted to the Heads of the People,
by HENY MELTON, of Regent-street. With curious Woodcuts of the various styles of Hats worn at different periods.

Anecdotes of eminent and fashionable personages are given, and a fund of interesting information relative to the History of Costume and change of tastes may be found scattered through its pages.

This day, neatly printed, price 1s. 6d., by post 1s. 8d.,

Mental Exertion: Its Influence on Health. By Dr. BRIGHAM. Edited, with additional Notes, by Dr. ARTHUR LEARED, Physician to the Great Northern Hospital.

This is a highly-important little book, showing how far we may educate the mind without injuring the body. A chapter, full of interest, is given on the education of scientific and literary men, the excitement they live in, their health, and the age they generally attain.

The *recent untimely deaths of Admiral Fitzroy and Mr. Prescott, whose minds gave way under excessive* MENTAL EXERTION, *fully illustrate the importance of the subject.* The work is not written in a dry, scientific style, but is of that anecdotal and popular character which befits it for general perusal.

⁎⁎⁎ NOTE.—In order to insure the correct delivery of the ACTUAL WORKS, *or* PARTICULAR EDITIONS, *specified in this list, it is necessary that* THE NAME OF THE PUBLISHER SHOULD BE DISTINCTLY GIVEN, *otherwise the purchaser will probably receive books of a different character from those which were ordered.*

☞ *A Catalogue of Interesting and Curious Books may be had gratis.*

JOHN CAMDEN HOTTEN,
74 AND 75, PICCADILLY, LONDON, W.

www.ingramcontent.com/pod-product-compliance
Lightning Source LLC
Chambersburg PA
CBHW020257170426
43202CB00008B/407